THE SAINT AN₁

CAMERON ₊

Saint Andrews Cathedral west door

For Fiona

THE SAINT ANDREW'S WAY

The modern restoration
of a medieval pilgrimage walk
from central Edinburgh
across the Forth Road Bridge
to St Andrews

CAMERON BLACK

Published by Cameron Black
E-mail: standrewsway@ymail.com

Copyright: © Cameron Black

The mapping is by David Langworth
(e-mail: david@maps.myzen.co.uk).
It is reproduced by permission of Ordnance Survey
on behalf of HMSO.   © Crown copyright 2010.
All rights reserved.   Licence number 100050107.

The public transport information (appendix),
the rear cover photo "Geese at sunset, Loch Leven"
and the two photographs on page 9
are provided by the courtesy,
and reproduced with the permission,
of Barry Cross.

ISBN: 978-0-9566500-0-9

FOREWORD

On 10th September 2000, David Simon's evocative painting in the National Gallery of Scotland of medieval pilgrims converging on St Andrews was mirrored as more than a thousand people, having arrived from all over Europe, *left* the Cathedral to retrace the route *back* across Fife. The reason behind this reversal was to arrive on 14th September – Holy Cross (or Holy *Rood*) Day – at another holy site, the precincts of Holyrood Abbey at the foot of Edinburgh's Royal Mile. Here HM The Queen had graciously given permission for an ecumenical millennium service to be held at her official Scottish residence. It marked the day on which King David had, whilst out hunting there in 1128, used a cross shaped stag's antlers to save himself from attack and, in relief, vowed to set up the abbey which was to give the place its historic name.

This modern pilgrimage was itself part of a greater millennium event, tracing a cross in Europe, from Thessalonika in the south, Trondheim in the north, Iasi in the east and a central climax in Prague. ***Action of Churches Together in Scotland***, through which mainstream churches co-operate, had been invited by the ***Conference of European Churches*** to offer a western 'arm' of this cross by reviving the medieval pilgrimage route across the Forth and Fife. King David's mother, Queen (Saint) Margaret of Scotland, had promoted the route a thousand years ago.

Before this renewing journey could begin, however, much preparation was needed to facilitate *Pilgrims Crossing Scotland 2000*, not least the charting of a viable modern route. It is here that the experience and enthusiasm of Cameron Black was indispensible. He applied himself to the task with unparalleled knowledge, skill and dedication, working with local authorities, land owners, *Historic Scotland* and other agencies to produce a pathway in sections that could be managed in five days.

The pilgrimage was organised to enable people to join in at any stage and by any means of transport. Not many of the long crocodile of people of all ages processing out of St Andrews that day walked the entire route; but Cameron was among those who did, having already tested the way. At every stopping point, again reviving ancient customs, local communities offered imaginative hospitality and their own style of pilgrim festival; at Ceres, Falkland and Dunfermline as well as St Andrews and Edinburgh. Anyone in the foreseeable future who walks the Way and stays at the places suggested in this book may hear of feasts and concerts, mystery plays, art exhibitions and craft fairs, and of an intrepid band who carried a cross 71 miles through typical September Scottish weather.

They may even hear of the after-event when, on St Andrew's Day 2000, a ferry was chartered to re-enact the crossing from Queensferry – the name comes from the largesse of Saint Margaret, who endowed free passage for medieval pilgrims to cross the Forth. On this day the Millennium Cross was erected on Inchgarvie Island, now nestling under the famous railway bridge but in the 11th century a mid-way pilgrim sanctuary. This cross is clearly visible to modern travellers by any means.

Cameron has since done much more research to chart the route in its original medieval direction and to make this guide accurate for continuing generations of explorers. It is written in his own witty style that characterised his contribution to "journeys of discovery where past and future are reconciled". It is as essential as a map for any proposing to walk The Saint Andrew's Way, and enjoyable as well as informative reading.

Rodney Matthews MBE
Co-ordinator, Pilgrims Crossing Scotland 2000

ACKNOWLEDGEMENTS

Three persons deserve especial mention: (1) Rev Rodney Matthews MBE who was Co-ordinator for Pilgrims Crossing Scotland 2000 and, without whose energy and inspiration, this book would never have appeared. (2) Alison Irvine who, as Access Officer for Fife, is most highly regarded by long distance walking authorities the length and breadth of the land, and was charged with producing the County of Fife's Core Path network plan whilst finding time to nudge your author in the best direction. (3) David Langworth who, with consummate skill, produced the maps herein and whom many of you already know, having used his maps – for walking or cycling – from the north of England to the Cairngorm Mountains.

Others, who provided information and/or were inspirational and/or went walking, are: Christine Davis, Sir Jack Stewart-Clark, Ninian Crichton Stuart, Patrick Laughlin, Peter Yeoman, David Watt, Dr Simon Taylor, Rev Dr Russell Barr, Jay and Jimmie Spankie, Nancy MacLeod-Nicol, Anne and Graeme Boyne, Kate Wheaton, Jim Kelly, Linda Fraser, Rosanna Cecchini, Rev Alasdair Elders, Morris Thomson, Jonathan Burrows, Simon and Kate Lidvell, Rev Matthew Ross, Ian White, Jim Nicholson, Rev Berit Lånke, Andrew Dyson, Tom Titterton, Jo Doake, Sandy Valentine, Donald Mackay, Neil Ramsay, Cathy Kinnear, Donald Murdoch, Neil Lobley, Uwe Stoneman, Andrea Habeshaw, Alan Graham, Roger Smith, Jock MacGillivray, Phillipa Parish, Jim Strachan, Ian and Anne Hendrie, George Reid, Michael and Helen Dick, Warren Hope, Richard Adlington, Margaret and Willie Deas, Margaret Morrison, Jo Reegan, Leonard and Diana Hart, Judy Arrowsmith, Terry Large, Doris Duncanson, Min Hunter, Tom and Maureen Borthwick, Tom and Agnes Notman, Alan Trotter, Heather and Tim Lees, Keith and Kay Frost, Margaret Armstrong, Flora Douglas, Keith and Morag Black, Barry and Diane Cross, Gavin Black, Donald Black, Fiona Black, Dr Gillian Black, Callum Black, Jim Duffy, Charles Jencks, Janet Stewart, Jean Paterson, Simon Gillam, Neil Bristow, Tina Hilder, Ann and David McCutcheon, Anne Wallace, Ruth Hems, Roger and Margaret Barr, Peter Inglis, David Low, Martina Piewald.

Raring to go! © Barry Cross

Which way now? © Barry Cross

9

CONTENTS

North Queensferry

Margaret's (2nd last) resting place at Dunfermline Abbey

INTRODUCTION

This is my *third* book about this walking route. The first was produced for a limited readership in the year 2000 for latter day pilgrims celebrating the second millennium. The second book was a simpler version of *this* edition – but with no maps – and appeared, privately, in 2003.

The first part of the present book, "Talk the Talk", allows me to ramble on about medieval pilgrimage in general and about Saint Andrew's shrine in particular; then to tell you about celebrations in the years 2000 and 2001; and, finally, to give some background to this exciting new version of a very ancient journey.

The second part of the book, "Walk the Walk", allows *you* to ramble on – all 115 kilometres (71 miles) to St Andrews. I just tell you something about how to get there and where to stay, leaving *you* to find out much more for yourself.

"What qualifications" I hear you cry "has this man got for patronising us in this manner?" I am a retired civil engineer with an interest in routes, generally, and paths in particular. My wife, Fiona, and I run the Cramond Walkers, so we know how to hurt your leg muscles and give you blisters *and* we have walked some long distance national trails, namely: The West Highland Way, The Speyside Way, St Cuthbert's Way, Offa's Dyke Path, and Hadrian's Wall Path. *This Way:* The Saint Andrew's Way, is a gem. Enjoy it.

> Now may this little book a blessing be
> To those who use this little book, and see!
> And may its buyer have no cause to say,
> His money is but lost or thrown away; . . .

Adapted from the Introduction to Part II of "The Pilgrim's Progress"
by John Bunyan (1628 – 1688).

.

St Andrew's Way

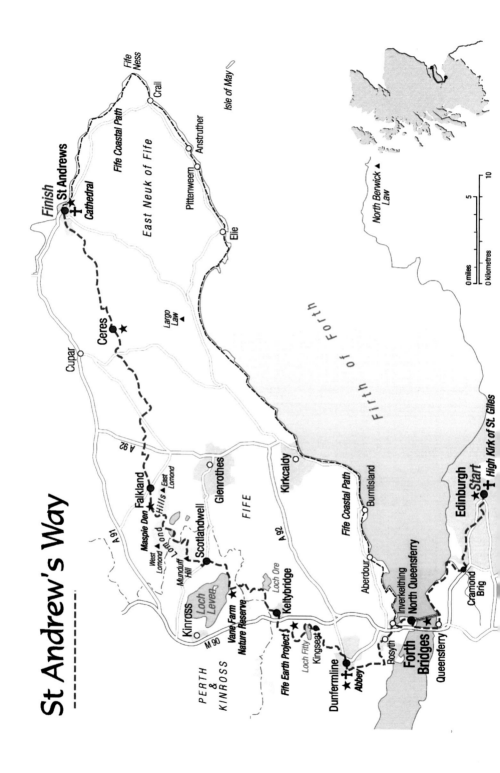

THE ST ANDREW'S WAY – DISTANCES

SECTION		Distance		Most Walkers:-		
		km	(miles)	Day	km	(miles)
1	Edinburgh (St Giles) to Cramond Brig	10	(6½)	1	24	(15)
2	Cramond Brig to North Queensferry	14	(8½)			
3	North Queensferry to Dunfermline	13	(8)			
4	Dunfermline to Kingseat	6	(4)	2	19	(12)
5	Kingseat to Keltybridge	8	(4½)			
6	Keltybridge to Vane Farm (RSPB)	8	(5)	3	21	(12½)
7	Vane Farm to Scotlandwell	5	(3)			
8	Scotlandwell to Falkland	14	(8½)	4	14	(8½)
9	Falkland to Ceres	21	(13)	5	21	(13)
10	Ceres to St Andrews (Cathedral)	16	(10)	6	16	(10)
	Totals	115	(71)	6	115	(71)

If you want a more gentle schedule, you could tackle the ten sections in eight days, combining sections 4+5: 14km (8½ miles) and combining 6+7: 13km (8 miles).

Very fit, enthusiastic walkers can do the whole walk in three days. Thus: Sections 1 to 3: 37km/(23 miles). Sections 4 to 8: 41km/(25 miles). On the third day – Sections 9 and 10: 37km/(23 miles).

PART ONE

TALK THE TALK

MEDIEVAL PILGRIMAGE

We revere our ancestors.　We take comfort from the past. We erect tombstones.　We visit graves.　We have war memorials and books of remembrance.　We put up statues. We learn from the past and find our direction for the future.

The early church helped this process by nominating saints and building shrines to some of them.　The faithful could visit a shrine, offer prayers, offer money, and – with luck and good timing – see the saint's relics.　The "goodness" of the saint would "rub off" on the worshipper.　Relics were sometimes kept in a box, to be revealed on the saint's day – his *holy day*. People would try to visit *on that day*, taking time off work with their boss's and their priest's approval, and so this was the start of the annual ***holiday.***

You would need holiday money.　Apart from food and lodging on the way, you'd want to offer money at the shrine (and the church would want you to) especially if you were seeking a cure from some disease or ailment.　Furthermore, you could purchase a shorter time in purgatory from a published tariff, allowing your soul to move on into heaven as soon as possible.

SAINT ANDREW'S SHRINE

Here we are, walking to Saint Andrews and there is *no* shrine! We have to rely on history and scenery: and what great things there are to see!   But first: the history.

The town of Saint Andrews' original name was Kinrymont: the "ry" bit signifying "king" because it was the seat of Pictish kings and the reason Fife is a "kingdom".   It may have been Bishop Acca (a known relic collector) who came north from Northumbria about 746AD bearing with him the very relics (well *alleged relics*) of one of Christ's apostles Saint Andrew, the brother of Peter.   The *official story*, however, was that a monk called Rule or, in Latin, Regulus, as the result of a vision in 345AD, brought the relics over from Andrew's shrine in Patras in Greece.   You may well say, when I tell you that the relics were an arm bone, three fingers, a knee-cap, and a tooth, "where are the other bits?"*   But of course that is not the point.   The point is: it was all a roaring success.

(1)   Several churches were built on the site – up to seven, perhaps, all at the one time.   You can still see, at least a part of, St Rule's Church with its tall tower which you can climb to relish the views from the top.   Outside the cathedral precinct wall – between it and the sea cliff – you can see the cruciform foundation of the early Culdee church, Saint Mary on the Rock.   It had got lost under the grass and was rediscovered in 1860.   The Culdees (it means Called by God) had come from Ireland where God seems to have omitted to mention that priests are not supposed to get married and raise children. The lovely bit is that the Culdee priests (13 of them) lived with their wives and families, in happy harmony with the celibate Roman priests who arrived later.   That is, until someone told tales and the Vatican put a stop to family life!

(2)   Andrew, whose relics were kept in St Rule's Church before the cathedral existed, became patron saint of Scotland, an important political move both for the feeling of national well-being and for the security of the monarch.

* I shall say more about "the other bits" later in this book.

(3)   The cathedral was completed – in a bit of a hurry – after the 1314 battle of Bannockburn.   It was consecrated in the presence of Robert the Bruce. It was the largest building in medieval Scotland and was built, perhaps deliberately, twelve metres longer than the only other cathedral in western Europe to hold an apostle's relics: those of Saint James, namely Santiago de Compostela in Spain.   Was it a case of "Come and see *ours*, it's bigger than *theirs*!'"?

(4)   Extra feast days allowed the crowds to access the relics and maximised Cathedral income.   The town moved from Royal seat, to religious centre, to university town, and golfing centre.   And people like you and me are *still hiking there!*

"Where" you may ask "did Cameron Black learn all this?"   For several years, I took Sunday School children from Cramond Kirk to visit Saint Andrews because its other claim to fame was as a centre of the Scottish Reformation.   John Knox preached in the town.   He and the Protestants had two main objectives: First: you should worship *one* God;   not saints' relics.   Secondly: payments for "indulgencies" were wrong.   The local people sacked the cathedral, destroyed the relics, removed lead from the roof, and used the stone as a free quarry over many years.   When *you* visit the site, you will already have passed half the stonework in buildings along the street, before you enter the cathedral gates!

I   recommend   your   reading   Peter   Yeoman's   book "Pilgrimage in Medieval Scotland" published by Batsford in 1999 but currently out of print (2009).

THE YEAR 2000

Notwithstanding ancient pilgrimages, this walk would never have been set up without "European Pilgrimage 2000", an initiative by the World Council of Churches. Representatives of the Conference of European Churches and the Roman Catholic Bishops' Conference met in Graz, Austria, in 1997 and decided to mark the second millennium.

In 2000 AD, four pilgrimages formed a cross on the map of Europe: South: Thessaloniki, Greece; North: Trondheim, Norway; West: St Andrews, Scotland; and East: Iasi, Romania. In 2001, the first year of the new millennium, there was a central celebration in Prague, Czech Republic. But there was one happy accident: the western celebration *should have been in England.* Don't ask me, I don't know! But Action of Churches Together in Scotland (ACTS) picked up the dropped ball and ran for goal.

The first I knew of this was after a phone call from our friends, Heather and Tim Lees who, at that time, were hoteliers in Falkland, Fife. They politely informed us (my wife, Fiona, and me) that they had told two hotel guests that *I* was an expert at walking about Fife. Hmm, was I? I had been given a book "Fifty Fife Walks" and had walked all of them. (I had intended to stop at forty nine to avoid accusations of enthusiasm, but there you have it.) More importantly: who were the two guests? Pastor Theo Bachtold and his wife, from Zurich, had checked in – soaking wet – having walked all the way from St Andrews. Yes, they were Rodney Matthews' reconnaissance party. Rodney – you will be quick to grasp – was the Scottish Pilgrimage Coordinator, the very man who had just picked up that dropped ball and was running for goal. And yes again: Theo gave Rodney my number.

Within hours I was on Rodney's Steering Committee. My job was to write a walking guide for energetic pilgrims. Now, you may have thought, as I did, that the Christian Way was "Straight and Narrow", so it may have been with just a touch of whimsy that our Rodney entitled the book "One Way or Another".

But year 2000 was not just a walk.   Many pilgrims hardly walked a step.   Cars or private buses were popular.   Included in the many pilgrim events along the route were: a Medieval Tavern, a 15th century Morality Play, an 18th century Communion, Latin singing of Mass, the Capernaum Choir, a Lithuanian Choir, an Ian White Concert with Broughton High School Jazz, the Royal High School Community Choir, and a pilgrim ferry across the River Forth.

Two months after the September 2000 Pilgrimage, a small group attended a ceremony in the middle of the River Forth, when our pilgrim cross, carved from oak from Dundas Castle estate, Queensferry, was erected on an island at the base of one of the piers of the Forth Bridge (the railway one).   The date we chose for our celebration was Saint Andrew's Day: 30th November, 2000.

DEVELOPING THE ROUTE

*The **real** route development experts are the Fife Ranger
Service. I have particularly acknowledged the work by Alison
Irvine, Access Officer. The route was developed for 2000, but
was **so good** we just couldn't let it go – as it were – to waste!*

Surely we could use the historic pilgrim route?   Hang on a
minute.   First, your route depends on your starting point!
Secondly, for any starting point there are lots of choices of
route.   We know there were certain places pilgrims liked to
visit en route, hostels or hostelries for instance and certain
subsidiary shrines, but it is very doubtful if all pilgrims visited
all of them.   In fact it is certain they did not.   If medieval
pilgrims were like modern walkers, then minimum time,
minimum distance, and short cuts were all important.
However: if you were starting (as we are) from south of the
Forth, you had to cross the river – the nearest bridge being at
Stirling!   So you needed a boat.   Two ferries existed (both
now gone) an eastern crossing from North Berwick to
Earlsferry, and a western route from Queensferry to North
Queensferry which lasted until 1964 when the Forth Road
Bridge opened.

It is obviously easiest for us to choose the bridge at
Queensferry.   Original pilgrims often headed directly from
Queensferry to Scotlandwell, dodging Dunfermline.
However, Queen Margaret who had, after all, provided the
ferry (Queen's Ferry) was finally laid to rest in 1093 in
Dunfermline and her tomb became a shrine, itself.   Indeed,
after she was canonised, the Pope actually declared that
pilgrims seeking Saint Andrew *should* also visit Dunfermline.
My original route from Dunfermline to Scotlandwell passed
through Balingry and along a frankly dangerous stretch of
road.

Now, thanks to the understanding and kindness of the
Royal Society for the Protection of Birds (RSPB), who have
extended their protection to jay-walkers (sorry), we can now
come over Vane Hill to reach Scotlandwell safely – via
RSPB's café.

Getting away from Scotlandwell on the original route would, today, mean walking another lethal road, the one leading to Leslie - no footpaths and fast traffic. But the Lomond Hills beckoned. This means missing out Markinch and Kennoway, favoured by some pilgrims. But we benefit from a visit to Falkland and get back on track at Ceres, which we enter on a section of the old Bishop's road, which only got that name after Archbishop Sharp was murdered on it. There is a choice of ways into St Andrews and we've chosen a pretty one based on one of the ridge routes which were often safer to travel upon.

We initially avoided an open cast mine which should be landscaped by the start of 2013. From then we can walk through. We have also minimised road walking and some five sixths of the way is off public roads. We know, from having led many walkers, that some folk object to twists and turns. "We're not maintaining direction!" Others complain about losing altitude when, presumably, twisting and turning along a contour line would be preferable. But all walkers hate long straights! We have taken great care with our compromises and have tried to offer the scenery, surprises, and opportunities for serendipity which you all appreciate.

The Land Reform (Scotland) Act 2003 has helped immensely in decision-making. More of this is mentioned in the Walk the Walk part. Also: the records kept by the Scottish Rights of Way and Access Society (Scotways) have proved invaluable.

The 2000 route went the reverse way. At that time I made notes walking the route *both* ways to cater also for today. You wouldn't believe the braided pencil lines on my Fife maps. But we have chosen only one way!

21

FEATURES OF THE WALK

Have you ever wondered if, at the time of the Reformation, the Protestants did perhaps protest *too much*? Was there overkill? Or is "overkill" an over-statement? I am not really talking about concrete (or, um, stone) objects. Though, obviously it would be rather different visiting a complete and entire cathedral, rather than the remains of walls, and columns, with the odd arch or tower remaining, which we find on completing The Saint Andrew's Way. I am talking about *pilgrimage* itself. Was the baby thrown out with the bath water? I suggest you are about to find out! The act of walking – slowly – from A to B to C to D imparts to the pilgrim a powerful sense of *progress.* You have to complete a continuous walk, staying in a different place each night, to achieve this. Even if you already think you know Fife like the back of your hand you will *relish* seeing things from your new perspective and seeing many things you did not know about. You will experience camaraderie, even if you are walking alone. You may well make new friends. You may want to come back again. You may be surprised to find you gain unexpected respect from folk you meet: "Where are you from?" "I've just walked from Edinburgh." "You've WHAT?!!!!!" They only *pretend* you need your head examined. They're actually jealous of what you are achieving. Tell me at the end, if I'm wrong.

If you walk eight hours a day then, presumably, you're not moving much for the other sixteen hours. So, where you stop overnight is important. Sorry, you really can not find camp sites on this route. "Wild camping" may be possible if you do some careful planning but I have always made use of bed and breakfast places or hotels. B&Bs need nearby pubs for your evening meal. I do hope the future will bring additional B&Bs onto the route. I (being bone idle) tend to favour the reasonably priced hotel, where your shower, your bed, your meal, your bar, and your television for worrying about tomorrow's weather forecast are all under one roof. A vast amount of The Way's route planning has been to ensure overnight stops are practicable.

Now: a *lack of features* of the walk! Warning: at present (2009) there are **no** waymarkers. Mind you, I recall a wet morning on St Cuthbert's Way, when the entire group we were with marched past a prominent finger-post sign which pointed right. I was leading from the rear, so shouted "Stop!" then duly lectured about observation. Three kilometres later the entire group walked straight past a signed left turn. I waited at a bridge further on, knowing they'd have to cross it after wandering about a bit. I said nothing. The problem? You don't look up when its raining and you don't pay attention when you're chatting. Notwithstanding this, waymarkers do help, and, hopefully – one day – they will help. It all takes money.

Let's take The Saint Andrew's Way section by section.

In **Section 1**, we visit "The High Kirk of St Giles". When it was founded in the 1100s it was, of course Roman Catholic. After the Reformation in 1560, John Knox became its first minister; and it kept its roof! Courtesy of Charles I and Charles II, it *twice* became an Episcopal cathedral in the 1600s before reverting to Church of Scotland. Most folk still call it St Giles' Cathedral – though, technically, it is not.

From Edinburgh Castle Esplanade, we creep down a path, which remarkably few take: close in to the cliffs of the Castle rock. The big fountain we pass down in Princes Street Gardens was provided by the Caledonian Railway Company. The city fathers would not allow the thing to be erected up on the street at the West End (of Princes Street). Possibly just as well: try standing down wind on a breezy day. Only 600m north west of the West End, we find ourselves strolling by a sylvan stream.

Later, you can thank that same Caledonian Railway for bringing golfers to Barnton from 1895, allowing us to walk between the two golf courses which were established within the grounds of Barnton House.

23

Section 2 takes us over the 16th century Cramond Brig, noting the repair dates on the upstream parapet. Modern repairers are not allowed to carve their repair dates, because it is a "listed building" – partly because of the repair dates carved on the parapet wall! Don't you just love stuff (and nonsense) like this? Soon we follow the shore of the Forth Estuary to reach charming Queensferry; with North Queensferry across the bridge. You'll enjoy these villages.

The view in **Section 3**, as we leave North Queensferry is simply jaw-dropping. I do hope the weather is clear for you. Do include Inverkeithing Civic Centre café and, next door, the 13th/14th century Franciscan Friary with delightful gardens and ruins to the seaward side. The view from the top of the next rise, Muckle Hill, is similar to that enjoyed earlier – but from higher up.

Leaving Rosyth on a green lane leads us towards the interesting Douglasbank Cemetery with the pleasant and gentle Bell Hills, beyond.

You will relish the drama of our entry to Dunfermline by the banks of Tower Burn in Pittencreiff Park and then up, past (can we believe it?) the very ruins of Queen Margaret's and King Malcolm Canmore's actual house!

Section 4 takes us over Kingseathill with wide views to the south; and then over wooded Town Hill, and thence to Kingseat.

In **Section 5** stood the hamlet of Lassodie which vanished because of open-cast coal mining. In 2011, the present mining may stop on this site, and from 2013, we should all be walking through the landscaped Fife Earth Project designed by Charles Jencks, the notable architect. Until then, the Way goes round the east end of Loch Fitty, very pretty, and detours west round the mine. The distance table on p14 shows *future* distances – a bit shorter. (Ironically, the mine is called St. Ninian's; and St Ninian's church at Whithorn, in Galloway, was a place of pilgrimage for over a thousand years.) This section ends in the delightful little village of Keltybridge.

Section 6:   The bridge at Keltybridge *originally* carried the main road north, the route – now M 90 – was, pre motorway, what you will now find labelled the B 996.   We do join *this* former "Great North Road" a couple of fields and a water meadow beyond Keltybridge.

Presently, we find ourselves on the switchback of Harran Hill and the shoulder of the tautologically named Benarty Hill and about to *descend* to the top of Vane Hill, the magnificent view-point of the RSPB reserve.   Here we overlook Loch Leven where Mary Queen of Scots was imprisoned on Castle Island (1560s).   Historic Scotland run boat trips there from Kinross: another day, perhaps?

Section 7 could hardly be flatter, although there's a change of level when we take the pedestrian subway under the road which passes the RSPB centre.   After the rather surprising Loch Leven Sluice House, I'd have loved to take you via Levenmouth Farm on your way to Lochend Farm: but, unless and until such a route is opened up, we must follow the walking directions in the book.   Pilgrims were attracted to Scotlandwell.   Visit the well to find out why.   Can you see water bubbling up through the sand?

Walkers on top of Munduff Hill

25

Section 8, I have been told, has the ascent that gives The Saint Andrew's Way 'its teeth'. In 1.5 km (1 mile), horizontally, we ascend 340 m (over 1,000 feet). The *average* gradient is 1 in 4½. Once up, we amble across the gently undulating plateau of the Lomond Hills, past reservoirs and through woodland. A very agreeable time. From the low point (Highlanders would say 'bealach') between West Lomond and East Lomond, at Craigmead car park, we make our way down exciting Maspie Den towards Falkland and its Palace. The village regularly wins competitions for its floral displays.

The start to **Section 9** is as flat, on the River Eden plain, as Section 7 was by the River Leven, until – that is – we are past delightful Kingskettle. Then, from Balmalcolm it's up and up to the slopes of Down Law and Cults Hill. We pass some points of interest as we head up to Coaltown of Burnturk. Yes, there used to be mining here, too. From the heights, we enjoy a sweeping vista over the Eden Valley. It even sounds biblical – appropriate for pilgrims! From the road to Chance Inn we can peer down on the track bed of a former mine era railway. Chance Inn was a 'Change Inn' where they changed stage-coach horses, but there is no inn in sight today. Craigrothie has an inn, which I have not been lucky enough to find open. It does have an interesting ford, used by horses. Human pedestrians cross dry-shod on a narrow bridge, alongside. So, does this make it a pack horse bridge?

Ceres (locals say 'Seeriss') *does* have a pack horse bridge: see the display boards in the car park. What other village do you know with a war memorial to the battle of Bannockburn (1314)?! Read the words on it. It's worth it. Visit the folk museum, if you can.

For the final section, **Section 10**, I had to choose a route into St Andrews. Working backwards, we just *had* to enter the cathedral via South Street from the ancient West Port. And we *had* to come down the Lade Braes Walk. This route follows the Kinness Burn. The burn had been dammed and a water channel formed to power mills and to supply the religious precincts with water. This was the mill lade. It cut across sloping gardens: the braes. Long since covered over for safety and greatly extended from the town centre (you'll find a commemorative stone) it is a lovely way to come into town.

From that old bridge in Ceres, the Bishop's Road went via the line of the modern road to Pitscottie and is then tricky to follow (I can assure you) though the line is shown on the ordnance survey 1:25,000 scale map. Our way makes use of a route via Kininmonth Hill and thence on quiet roads from Arnsheen past Denhead to a footpath via the entrance to Craigton Country Park – great fun for kids of all ages – then by way of 'the Den' which becomes 'Lumbo Den' feeding down into the Lade Braes Walk and town.

From the top of Kininmonth Hill it is generally downhill – an inevitable result of approaching a coastal town from inland! **Do keep your eyes peeled for a distant view over the town and cathedral which will make you imagine you are a pilgrim of yester year.**

The Author, his wife Fiona, with Anne and Ian Hendrie

27

The Water of Leith – Section 1

Douglasbank Cemetery – Section 3

Peacock at Dunfermline Palace – Section 3

28

Irony at Scotlandwell – Section 7

Ascending Munduff Hill – Section 8

Going down Maspie Den – Section 8

West Lomond from Harperleas Reservoir – Section 8

Maspie Den, behind the waterfall – Section 8

Kingskettle – Section 9

30

Ceres Bridge – Section 9

West Port, St Andrews – Section 10

31

PREPARING TO GO

Because my wife, Fiona, and I have led the Cramond Walkers for several years, we have picked up some pointers which – if walking is a bit of a novelty for you – may be of some use. Let us concentrate on three things:

(a) knowing that you *can* walk;
(b) knowing *where* you are going;
(c) knowing *what* to wear and carry.

Crossing the Forth Road Bridge

(a) *Can* you walk? If you are a bit inexperienced, you may worry about the daily distance. You may think 5km (2 or 3 miles) are ok. 10km (5 to 7 miles) may seem, perhaps, just about possible. 15 to 20km (10 to 12 miles) may sound a bit far. 25km (15 miles) must be really scary! If you recognise yourself in any of this, you would benefit from some practice walks. Choose a sunny day. Take a picnic. Take a friend. Go somewhere pleasing. Enjoy the outdoors. Check how far you went by using a map.

Inexperienced walkers may get blisters or sore bits. If you get blisters, you need more walking practice to toughen your feet and/or your footwear is not appropriate. Carry a first aid kit including magic artificial skin, from the chemist, for mending blisters.   Walking boots or shoes *must* be comfortable. Two pairs of socks are a good idea. Take advice.

Longer distances may give pains behind your shins or hurt your thighs. Regular walkers don't get sore bits, they just get tired. *When you can walk without blisters, sore bits, or worrying, you are ready.* The good news is that the fit walker can walk all day, every day. Aren't we wonderful?

Perhaps, as you walk, you start thinking 'When will we get there?' or 'Are we nearly there?' The rule which Cramond Walkers use is that walking groups go remarkably slowly! If you allow 1 hour for 3km (or 2 miles) which includes an allowance for coffee stops and admiring the view, you will be in the right ball park. There are more complex formulae available – useful if different parties are to rendezvous at a certain place – but, using our simple rule, the distance from Edinburgh (St Giles) to North Queensferry is 24km (15 miles). So, allow 8 hours (or 7½ hours!). For nit-pickers: the ½ hour difference is because 3km are only *approximately* 2 miles. You will notice I have selected the *longest* distance, namely 'day 1', from the 'Most Walkers' column in the Distances table. Unless your 'day 1' is to include a very leisurely lunch, a 9am start means a 5pm finish. Then, you will find that 'day 2' represents 6 hours (10am to 4pm). Easy – eh?

(b) *Where* are you going?   David Langworth's maps are excellent, but don't expect a coloured line on the ground to conduct you all the way to St Andrews! If you want to compare David's maps with Ordnance Survey maps, you'll need to buy or borrow four. I prefer 'Explorer' 1:25,000 scale maps, because the large scale shows more details – such as fence lines. The maps required are numbers 350, 367, 370, and 371. [You'd still need four maps at the smaller scale of 1:50,000: maps numbered 58, 59, 65, and 66.] A small proportion of the Way is on road. More usually, we are on well-defined path; but one or two bits are ill-defined – on hillside or across fields. Until kind people put up way-markers and the Way becomes established, you should rely heavily on reading the text. May I suggest that it is easier to read ahead than to walk back?!

33

The directions have been tested. I am not going to say 'idiot-proofed', because our very good friends Ian and Anne Hendrie did the testing and we want to *remain* friends and, for all I know, they are as smart as you are. They *led* my wife and me along the entire Way to St Andrews! Thank you both. Since then, I have accompanied two other groups along the entire Way, to gauge reaction. I am strongly confident in offering you The Saint Andrew's Way. This is a great route to cut your teeth on, and a splendid east of Scotland counterbalance to the west of Scotland's West Highland Way. You'll even find lochs and hills, but – probably – fewer showers!

In Scotland, we enjoy the right of access to land as set out in the Land Reform (Scotland) Act 2003, which came into force in 2005. So far as I can ascertain, you have a right to be on any point of The Saint Andrew's Way. (Two public parks: Princes Street Gardens, Edinburgh and Pittencrieff Park, Dunfermline may – though it is unlikely – be closed when you arrive, but the book gives diversions.) Otherwise the keywords are 'respect' and 'responsibility'. You are *required* to respect the interests of others, for example land managers, and to take responsibility for your own actions. Your dog has similar rights of access provided it is under 'proper control'. A principal effect of this legislation has been to give walkers a greater confidence. 'Tolerance' is the new watchword.

For reasons I cannot foresee, this walk, and any walk, may sometimes require walkers to divert, requiring the application of initiative and other maps. Just be prepared. I have minimised 'hostage-to-fortune' directions. The white house mentioned in Queensferry will doubtless be blue or red when you get there – or demolished. At least, I have not asked you to turn left when you come to the field of brown cows. I have tended to say *'you'* *do this* when it helps to focus your attention, and I may choose *'we'* *go along here* to make you feel I'm there with you, looking after you! I just hope this technique works.

(c) *What* should you wear and carry? Would it be too obvious to state: take the stuff you need but don't carry unnecessary weight? Your boots/shoes should be *waterproof.*

34

Your jacket (with a hood) should be *waterproof* and should *breathe*.   Waterproof trousers are a good idea – even as protection against brambles, nettles, prickles, or just long, wet, grass.   Gloves, scarf, and a pullover are good to have.   Dry socks are vital – fresh daily – but can be washed;   likewise, underwear.   Three shirts: two for walking, on alternate days, and one for evenings, will keep down weight.   Take money.   You'll find cash machines in – at least – Edinburgh, Rosyth, Dunfermline, Falkland, and St Andrews.

Your rucksack should fit comfortably, with cross straps at waist and chest.   It should be waterproof or contain a waterproof bag.   Take water/flask, food, torch, compass/GPS, phone (loaded with the numbers you'll need), camera, midge repellent (for June to September).   Take this book!   And *keep it dry!*

The weather in Scotland is temperate.   The rainfall in the east, where The Saint Andrew's Way lies, is about *half* that in the west.   You really can walk at any time of the year, but remember: daylight is short in mid winter (about 9.15am to 3.30pm) and walking on ice is slippery and can be dangerous unless you are properly prepared.   Good months are often around May or September.   Check web sites.

To return from St Andrews, buses leave for Edinburgh at regular intervals.   The bus station is off City Road, about 200m north from West Port.   Again: check web sites.   See Barry Cross's appended Public Transport Information, p80.

The bottom line is that you are responsible for yourself!

35

ACCOMMODATION

No doubt, someone will set themselves up in the business of finding your accommodation and carrying your cabin trunk along the Way. In the meantime, we must make our own arrangements. I, who have walked the *entire* Way on three occasions, have – I am almost surprised to realise – used three rather different techniques:

(a) I stayed at a different place each night, carrying *all* my kit.

(b) Similar; but with a kit-carrying vehicle.

(c) *Commuting:* I stayed two nights in Edinburgh, one in Dunfermline, and three in Falkland with a group who had access to a 12-seater Land Rover.

(a) or (b) are simpler to organise and more satisfying to complete. The problem with (c) is persuading your pick-up to meet you at the right time and place when it's raining and getting dark! Just remember that, once you have booked your accommodation, you have set up a contract with the other party. It may be costly *and* discourteous to fail to turn up. I now offer you a list of places, thirteen of which we have used.

Edinburgh   (Here is one of the many places available)
Castle Rock Hostel, 15 Johnstone Terrace (Close to Castle)
     OS Ref NT 255735   Tel 0131 225 9666
Queensferry
Hawes Inn. (By the Forth [rail] Bridge. On the Way)
     OS Ref NT 138784   Tel 0131 331 1990
Priory Lodge Guest House, 8 The Loan   (By the Way)
     OS Ref NT 129783   Tel 0131 331 4345
North Queensferry
The Queensferry Hotel. (N end of bridge. On the way)
     OS Ref NT 125809   Tel 01383 410 000
Ferrybridge Hotel. (Beside Forth [rail] Br. On the Way)
     OS Ref NT 132805   Tel 01383 416 292
Battery House B&B. 3 East Bay. (300m from Way)
     OS Ref NT 134804   Tel 01383 410 163
Dalwhinnie B&B. 10 East Bay. (400m from Way)
     OS Ref NT 135803   Tel 01383 410 457

Dunfermline
City Hotel, Bridge St.   (E of High St.   100m from Way)
   OS Ref NT 089875   Tel 01383 722 538
Kingseat
Half Way House Hotel.   (On the Way)
   OS Ref NT 125904   Tel 01383 731 661
Lochfitty Cottage B&B.   (On B912, 450m from Way)
   OS Ref NT 131915   Tel 01383 831 081
Kelty
Thistledome B&B.   (1km off the Way)
   OS Ref NT 138940   Tel 01383 830 119
Scotlandwell
Well Country Inn.   (On the Way)
   OS Ref NO 185016   Tel 01592 840 444
Falkland
Luigino's.   (Opposite fountain.   On the Way)
   OS Ref NO 253074   Tel 01337 857 224
Bruce Hotel.   (Opposite Palace.   On the Way)
   OS Ref NO 254074   Tel 01337 857 226
Freuchie
Lomond Hills Hotel.   (900m off the Way)
   OS Ref NO 283068   Tel 01357 857 329
Ceres
Meldrums Hotel.   (300m north from Way)
   OS Ref NO 399116   Tel 01334 828 286
St Andrews   (Here are some of many places available)
Yorkston House.   68-70 Argyle St.   (200m off Way)
   OS Ref NO 504166   Tel 01334 470 351
Best Western Scores Hotel,   The Scores.   (700m off Way)
   OS Ref NO 505170   Tel 01334 472 451
Castlemount B&B.   (Opposite Castle.   300m off Way)
   OS Ref NO 512169   Tel 01334 475 579
Abbey Cottage.   Abbey Walk.   (500m off Way)
   OS Ref NO 516164   Tel 01334 473 727

PART TWO

WALK THE WALK

THE WAY IN 10 SECTIONS, TAKING 'MOST WALKERS' 6 DAYS

ROUTE DESCRIPTIONS

ROUTE MAPS (Key on page forty)

Note: A suggestion for 'most walkers' is to combine Sections 1 & 2 on the first day;   then to combine Sections 3 & 4 on the second;   then Sections 5,6 & 7 on the third;   finally taking three days for the last three sections (at one section per day).

SECTION 1

EDINBURGH (ST GILES)
TO CRAMOND BRIG: 10km (6½ miles)

If you are a first time visitor to the capital of Scotland – which is host to the international festival and military tattoo – I hope you will already agree it seems such a shame to walk away from this 'Athens of the North' to explore further afield.   You will just have to come back and linger longer!   From the end of this first, shortish, section you can readily get a bus back to the city centre in about half an hour, and you can just as easily return for Section 2 tomorrow.   In today's introductory offering: on leaving the High Street and after strolling down through Princes Street Gardens, we follow the Water of Leith, tramp a former railway route, walk between two golf courses and cross an ancient bridge over the River Almond.

But first: let's get to the start!
    We have to get to the High Kirk of St Giles in the "High Street" (at Ordnance Survey Ref. NT 257736).   If you arrive in Edinburgh at the bus station or the train station, these are conveniently close.   From the bus station, exit towards "St Andrew Square" (appropriate name).   Turn left on the street to get to "Princes Street", where you turn right, then *immediately left* into "Waverley Bridge" – soon passing the train station.   If you have arrived by train, take the Waverley Bridge exit.   Here you turn left, tagging along behind the bus passengers.   Now, we are all marching away from Princes Street and we're facing the great bulk of hillside on which the Old Town is built.   In fact, we have just realised what "High" in "High Street" means!   Go ahead into "Cockburn Street" then *turn first right up some steps into **"Advocate's Close"**.* Simply follow this uphill: St Giles is in front of you at the top.   Go in the west (uphill) door and have a look around (coffee shop, downstairs).

39

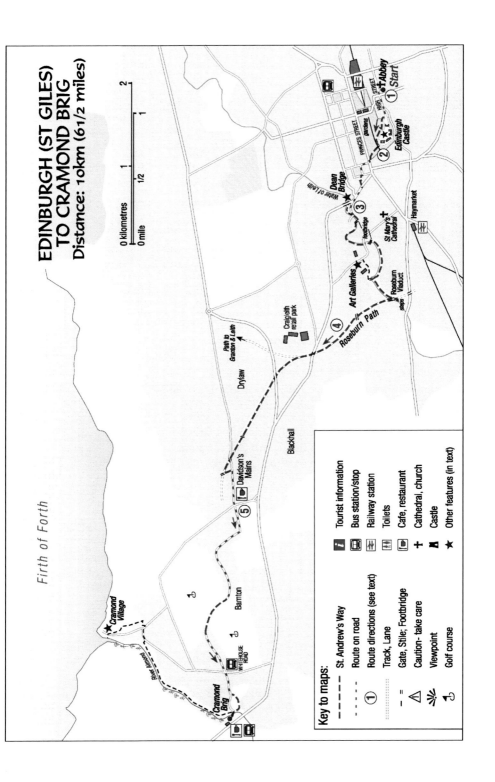

EDINBURGH (ST GILES) TO CRAMOND BRIG
Distance: 10km (6 1/2 miles)

Firth of Forth

0 kilometres   1/2   1   2
0 mile   1/2   1

★ Cramond Village

River Almond

★ Cramond Brig

Barnton

WHITEHOUSE ROAD

Davidson's Mains

⑤

Blackhall

Drylaw

Path to Granton & Leith

Craigleith retail park

④

Roseburn Path

Roseburn Viaduct   steps

Art Galleries ★

footbridge

St Mary's Cathedral ✝

③

Haymarket

Dean Bridge ★

Water of Leith

PRINCESS STREET

② Edinburgh Castle

gardens

HIGH STREET

① Start ✝ Abbey

Key to maps:

- - - - -   St. Andrew's Way
————   Route on road
①   Route directions (see text)
— =   Track, Lane
= =   Gate, Stile; Footbridge
......   Caution- take care
⚲   Viewpoint
⛳   Golf course

ℹ   Tourist information
🚌   Bus station/stop
🚉   Railway station
🚻   Toilets
🍴   Cafe, restaurant
✝   Cathedral, church
🏰   Castle
★   Other features (in text)

Now, let's walk: Use the Map.

(1)   Leave St Giles by the main, west, door. Outside, look for the Heart of Midlothian marked in setts on the ground near the carriageway (right).   It denotes the site of the former tollbooth prison, and our freedom!   Keep walking up the "High Street" – it is more convenient to be on the right hand side – until you arrive on the castle esplanade.   **STOP!**   *As soon as you arrive on the esplanade, move to your right* and go through the gate just before a memorial monument, into public gardens with grass and trees.   [If gate locked, see "DIVERSION", below].   Otherwise, follow the path.   At a path junction, bear right to keep going down.   Keep going down, *always keeping as close as possible to the castle rock face (left).*   Using this rule, you presently enter a ruin: BIG STEP DOWN!   Join the path by the railway (keeping the railway on your right.

(2)   Turn right to cross the railway by a bridge.   Walk ahead, bearing *gently* left at forked junctions.   (Pass a play area, left).   Head up to a broad flight of steps leading to "Princes Street".   Cross Princes Street at the traffic lights (just to your left) to enter "South Charlotte Street".

[DIVERSION: If the gate from the esplanade is locked, go back down the street, but turn first left down "Ramsay Lane".   At bus route, turn left and see if you can enter gardens through a pedestrian gate – leading to the path by the railway – or turn left into Princes Street then third right into "South Charlotte Street".]

Walk up South Charlotte Street, crossing mouth of lane, and turn left to walk along south side of Charlotte Square.   At the next corner, cross the road towards the building with the large green (copper) dome and *start* walking along the next side of the square but dodge left down an alley immediately before the building with the dome.   At far end, go right then left into "Randolph Place".   At main road (bus route), turn right *but it is best to walk on the left hand side.*   Where the main road curves right, you must cross the closed-off mouth of "Belford Road", then:-

(3)   Dive left down "Bell's Brae" – "Leading to Dean Village".   At crossroads, detour right into "Miller Row" to stop and view Thomas Telford's Dean Bridge (A90 to Fife).

41

Telford was the first president of the Institution of Civil Engineers.   Return to crossroads and go ahead into "Hawthornbank Lane" (sign "Balerno 9").   Pass a stone bollard.   Go down to, and cross, footbridge over Water of Leith.   On opposite bank, circle round to your right to pass under the footbridge and head upstream (water on left). Follow the riverside path, ignoring junctions.   Only cross the river once, *after* passing under a stone arched road bridge. Eventually, the high Roseburn railway viaduct is seen ahead (NT 231734).   Go under it and *immediately,* at sign "North Edinburgh Cycleway", **turn left** up 85 steps.   Turn left to cross the viaduct.

The way in Dean Village

(4)   Follow the cycleway for some 3km (2 miles).   After you pass the overgrown platforms of the former Craigleith Station (access to A 90), you come to a cycleway junction. We must fork left (sign "Queensferry 7 and Forth Road Bridge 7½") on National Cycle Route No 1.   At the top of a long straight, our path goes under a stone bridge, then under a steel one, *then,* just before the next bridge (NT 209756), the cycle route *swings right away from the railway.*   **Just here, take the flight of steps up to the top of the bridge**.   Turn left at the top and cross the bridge.   At the main road, turn right to walk straight through Davidson's Mains village.   (Pub on left; another on right;   but popular locally is "The Village Tea

Room" located down the last road on the left, at a mini roundabout.)

(5)   Continue *straight ahead* at the end of Main Street, between old stone gate pillars, the former east entrance to Barnton House (demolished).   Follow road round to right, passing Royal High School entrance, then go *straight ahead* at main road ("Cramond Brig 1½, Queensferry 4½").   Soon, the road becomes a path between golf courses, reverting later to road.   Cross Whitehouse Road, still following cycle route, into "Braepark Road".   [Note: buses to town use Whitehouse Road, crossing our Way from right to left].   Where the valley, carrying Braepark Road downhill, opens out, *turn left* onto a track (with field on right), to pass a play park (left).   At path junction, turn right to return to road.   Turn left and cross old Cramond Brig.   (Note the repair dates on the upstream parapet.)

This is the end of Section 1, but note that "The Cramond Brig Pub and Dining Rooms" are over the bridge on the left.   Also over there, the main A 90 road has more buses back to town.

The Water of Leith

43

SECTION 1: AN APPENDIX

A NOTE ABOUT CRAMOND

Pilgrims had to ford the river, either at Cramond Brig (Scots for 'Bridge') or near the mouth of the river. At both sites, the river is now deeper. A weir to provide a head of water for mills, downstream of the bridge, has deepened the water but provided a tranquil view from the bridge. At Cramond, a 'bar' across the river keeps Club members' boats afloat at low tide, so you'd have difficulty fording now. In any event the crossing could only be made here at low tide, so the Dalmeny Estate provided a toll ferry for nearly 400 years – until 2001.

You modern pilgrims may (one day) have to be alert for a new river crossing at Cramond! Edinburgh Council have given approval, in principle, to a new footbridge near the foot of School Brae (more about the location, below). Others have proposed a daytime-only chain ferry for pedestrians and bicycles, sited closer to the river- mouth, by the boat moorings. In the meantime, I shouldn't hold my breath if I were you.

The directions which follow, give 'short day 1' walkers (i.e. Section 1 only) the opportunity of adding a visit to Cramond Village onto their walk to Cramond Brig. It also gives directions to the new crossing – when available.

Cramond Brig

44

Cramond Brig to Cramond Village: 2km (1½ miles) *one way.*

Having admired the view from Cramond Brig, retrace your steps off the bridge but turn first left into "Dowie's Mill Lane" to follow the riverside road/path.   After the river gorge (steps up and steps down) and beyond a waterfall, fork right on a road leading uphill.   (The bridge – if built – would be near this road and would take you up to point (2) on the next map, where you'd turn right to the Shore Path).   Otherwise, at the top of the uphill road, go left (buses to town are across the road) and soon cross the mouth of "Cramond Glebe Road" and bear round to the right.   **But, in 20m, turn left into a footpath** and pass metal barriers.   Go round bends, bearing left, and, after two walled enclosures, emerge in a car park. Maintain the same direction and pause at the far end of the building (which you've passed on your right).

Cramond House is on your right.   Cramond Tower, once the residence of the bishops of Dunkeld, is ahead of you.   Our way turns left towards a gate in Cramond Kirkyard.   **Before** the gate, fork right onto the *Via Principalis* and the Roman fort interpretation panel.   Some stones in the church have criss-cross grooves – originally worked by Roman masons in 142 AD.   'Cramond' means 'The Fort by the Water'.   The first two letters, originally 'Caer', are from Caere an Etruscan fortified town north of Rome; and '-amond' derives from *aqua* 'water'.   Where the *Via Principalis* meets the tarmac drive, turn **right** and, at the passing place, turn left onto a path which has another panel giving the real age of Cramond inhabitants! At the foot of the path, go out to the roadway leading down into the village but, before a coffee shop, turn left down a flight of steps to the promenade.   (A ferry – if provided – would be near here.)

Otherwise, the road will take you up to those buses to town.

SECTION 2

CRAMOND BRIG
TO NORTH QUEENSFERRY: 14km (8½ miles)

For a flavour of what's in store: you'll soon be walking by the shore of the River Forth Estuary. You'll pass Eagle Rock carved – the story has it – by the Romans in about 142 A.D. when they were in residence at Cramond Fort. Cramond = Caer Amon = Fort by the Water (little imagination!) This part of the walk is a mixture of shore, woodland, and golf course. You'll find Dalmeny House, the home of Lord Rosebery and Hound Point with its wonderful estuary views. Pass through Queensferry and you are high above the water on the half hour stroll across the Road Bridge, before ending this section in the delightful village of North Queensferry. Queen Margaret, wife of King Malcolm Canmore, is remembered in the name "Queen's Ferry". She died in 1093 and her son King David I instituted the regular ferry service which continued in various forms until the road bridge opened in 1964.

Let's Walk! Use the Map.
    (1) From Cramond Brig continue out of town, up past "The Cramond Brig Pub and Dining Rooms". Turn right at the top, through the estate gateway signposted cycle route 76. An information board inside the estate shows a plan of the cycle route to Queensferry. We shall follow the shore path option shown with small circles on the board. Follow the estate road which presently bends uphill to reach East Craigie Farm. Continue on the road, in an absolutely straight line for 800m (½ mile).
    (2) Here, cycle route 76 is signed to turn left *but we go ahead bearing fractionally right* to go downhill. Entering trees, you must fork left where the main (?) track curves right. This leads to the "Shore Walk". Turn left. In two minutes, notice Eagle Rock on the shore where you can read Historic Scotland's cautious plaque. Go round Snab Point (map) then past Long Green Cottages. Cross the cottage access road into a tree avenue. Cross the footbridge (map) and turn right,

passing wood a on your left, to follow above the shore to the end of the golf course.

(3)   Join a surfaced estate road (turn right) to pass Barnbougle Castle.   Soon, where the surfaced road curves left, bear half right on "Shore Walk".   Beyond a cottage, at the top of a rise check out the views from Hound Point (map). A few minutes further along the Way, you will have to concentrate to identify St Margaret's Well.   It lies just over a crest.   Look on your right for an encircling iron railing and old privet hedge.   Pilgrims of yester year are said to have paused here.   We must *not* drink the water!

By Saint Margaret's well

(4)   We leave Dalmeny Estate at Longcraig Gate.   Peer closely at Inch Garvie island (map) to spot the oak cross erected on a flat roof at the right hand, downstream, end. Modern pilgrims (I was there!) erected it on St Andrew's Day, 30 November 2000, as the finalé to Pilgrims Crossing Scotland 2000.   We can thank them (and me!) for the St Andrew's Way.   The Way passes below the rail bridge approach viaduct.   [Lazy walkers can catch a train from Dalmeny Station (map) to North Queensferry – follow sign.] Proper walkers follow shore along road.   (Men's toilet, right, before jetty. Ladies', left, in 50m.)

47

CRAMOND BRIG TO NORTH QUEENSFERRY
Distance: 14km (8 1/2 miles)

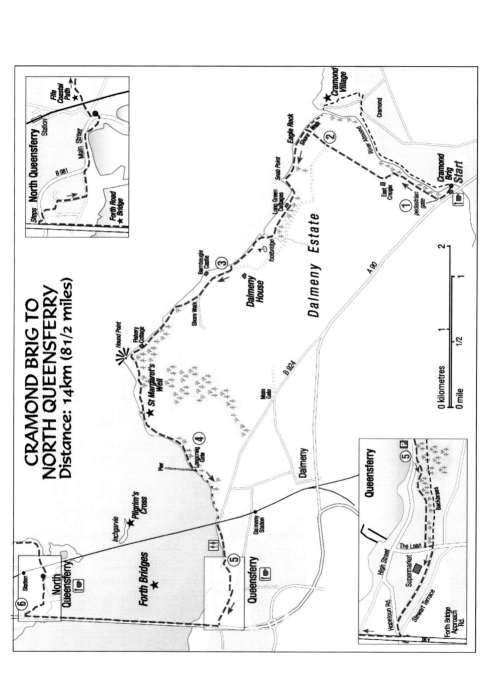

(5)   At the far end of the wide parking area, cross road to left and fork left, uphill.   Pass white villa (right) and bear right on main path. (Steps join from left.) Further along: at a fork, bear left, up, keeping 3-bar railing on your right.   At main road: cross; turn left uphill; but in 30m turn right into side road and walk on foot track along edge of carriageway. When this path splits, *keep left of railing* to avoid subway. At "Hopeton Road" turn left.   Cross mouth of "Stewart Terrace" and fork left up footpath/cycleway which goes under the Forth Road Bridge approach viaduct.   At roadway turn left and, at top, turn right to cross the Forth Road Bridge. You'll have a better chance to see the oak cross on Inch Garvie (map).   The wood came from Sir Jack Stewart-Clerk's Dundas Castle Estate.   He still owns the cross: it's on *his* island!   The cross symbolises 2000 years of Christianity and our own pilgrimage walk.   You're half way across when the main suspension cables reach their low point.   It's your *high* point!   You're as high above water as the top of Edinburgh's Scott Monument is above Princes Street.

(6)   At the end of the bridge, descend steps on right.   Turn left where route splits and go left to end of short footway. Cross road carefully and turn left.   At North Queensferry's welcome sign, turn right through gate.   Follow path into housing area and go directly down to shed door (Scottish Power's "Inchcolm Drive" sub station) and *turn left* up narrow path.   Turn right at street then left at main road.   Emerging from "Ferry Road", turn right into village.   As you are passing the bay, turn right at "public footpath" sign down onto short promenade.   Section 2 ends at the front of the Ferry Bridge Hotel, located at the village crossroads.   (OS NT 132805).

If you are staying in North Queensferry, you will find a short stroll round the town trail (notice boards) is well worth while. This takes you past the remains of a chapel dedicated to St James – the patron saint of pilgrims! Mind you, *this* chapel is a trifle smaller than the building in Santiago de Compostela in Spain!

SECTION 3

NORTH QUEENSFERRY
TO DUNFERMLINE (Abbey):   13km (8 miles)

[If you continue to Kingseat today, remember you'll be walking 19km (12 miles).]

The start of this section benefits from superlative views from the Fife Coastal Path section, moderated later by a scrap yard as we enter Inverkeithing!   Leaving Rosyth brings a welcome, rural, green lane character to the walk.   We enter Dunfermline town via delightful Pittencreiff Park from which Andrew Carnegie was ejected, as a boy.   Later, he bought it and gave it to the people.

Let's Walk!   Use the Map.

(1)   Start at the front door of the Ferry Bridge Hotel (NT 132805).   Head due north, to cross the mouth of "Old Kirk Road" towards a bell-shaped structure.   Turn right behind this object to follow "Fife Coastal Path" upwards.   Beyond a sandy beach, the outlook takes on an industrial quality as you come round to the Inner Bay of Inverkeithing (map).   Back on a surfaced road, walk on the right-hand footway.

(2) At a T-junction, turn right, but *in 30m, just **before** a low (4.0m headroom) bridge,* turn right again into a narrow footpath.   Beyond a large shed (right), your path deflects slightly to keep to the right hand side of a railway line.

Go up steps to a girder bridge and turn left to cross the railway line.   On the far side, follow the path up: stick to the main path.   At main road, turn right, uphill to visit Inverkeithing Civic Centre (toilets and café – open from 10.00 till 2.00).   Note: Just past this are the old hospitium – once handy for pilgrims - and charming adjoining gardens.   (I have, on your behalf, complained about the Fife welcoming signs: "No dog-fouling; no cycling; no ball games; no drinking of alcohol".)   On completion of your visit – if still sober, I suppose – cross the main road and turn left, downhill.

(3)   Very soon, at end of tenements, and *immediately past a bungalow with barred windows ("Lodge St John")* **turn right** up a narrow path.   Turn left on road at top and

50

immediately right on uphill road. On reaching a car-parking area at the top of the slope, keep going up, but bear left up a cobbled path (houses on left). At the top of this, turn right up 13 concrete steps. Go uphill on path, (grass on both sides), turning right in front of four lock-ups to continue uphill with a stone wall (right) and garden fences (left). At the top, turn right along road. At next main road (bus shelter opposite) turn left, soon crossing a bridge and turning right down "Castlandhill Road" (map).

(4) At the foot of the hill, the Way goes straight ahead at a roundabout. (Use the signalled crossing and make your way via tree-lined "Queensferry Road"). 600m along this road, use (the *second*) pedestrian crossing to reach the left hand side of the street where I can recommend the Palace Café's bacon rolls! (Closed Sundays.) Continue, now on left side of road, crossing "Aberlour Street" and passing a pay toilet. Turn left along "Park Road", continuing ahead at roundabout into "Park Road West". Turn first right into "Primrose Avenue" and follow round curves. Turn right by a bus shelter into "Anderson Lane" then, at main road, turn left and you can soon walk along the quieter service road.

(5) At cross-roads (where the main road turns left), our way goes ***straight ahead***, so cross carefully into a lane (cycle route). Continue ahead (map), then zig-zagging round buildings to Pattiesmuir (map) where you turn right and walk past cottages. At T-junction, turn right to pass Douglasbank Cemetery on a footpath. As you head uphill, the path heads towards a wood on the horizon: bear right on main path to reach this woodland. Go round woodland to the *right*, keeping wood on your left.

(6) On reaching a T-junction, turn right (map) towards Wester Gellet. At the farm buildings, turn left: then, at Limekilns Road (map), turn right. In Dunfermline, a road junction sign indicates car parks and Pittencreiff Park. Here, where "Forth Street" turns sharply right at a junction with "Milton Green" (left), our Way crosses the side road. ***Take care!***

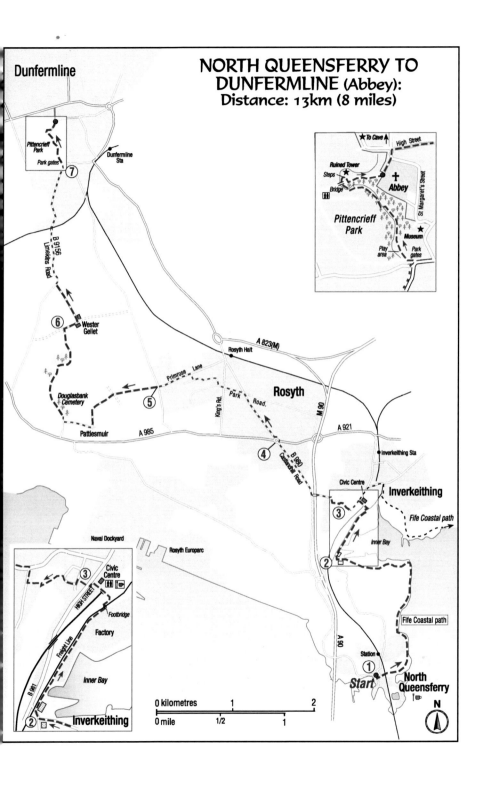

NORTH QUEENSFERRY TO DUNFERMLINE (Abbey):
Distance: 13km (8 miles)

Dunfermline

Pittencrieff Park

Park gates

⑦

Dunfermline Sta

B 9156 Limekilns Road

⑥ Wester Gellet

Douglasbank Cemetery

Pattiesmuir

A 985

⑤

Primrose Lane

King's Rd.

Park Road.

Rosyth Halt

A 823(M)

Rosyth

M 90

A 921

④

B 980 Castlandhill Road

Inverkeithing Sta

Civic Centre

③

Inverkeithing

Fife Coastal path

Inner Bay

②

Naval Dockyard

Rosyth Europarc

③ Civic Centre

HIGH STREET

Footbridge

Factory

Freight Line

Inner Bay

B 981

② Inverkeithing

Fife Coastal path

A 90

Station

① Start

North Queensferry

Inset (top right):

★ To Cave

High Street

Ruined Tower ★

Steps

Bridge

✝ Abbey

St. Margaret's Street

Pittencrieff Park

Museum ★

Play area

Park gates

0 kilometres   1   2

0 mile   1/2   1

N

(7)   Enter Park gates and *immediately turn right!* [If park closed, bear right to traffic signals.   Turn left, uphill.   Path ahead past grass area – old road line – then up to turn left into "Monastery Road" to west door of Abbey].   Otherwise, having turned right just inside Park gates, follow path past play area (left) until you are walking beside a stream (Tower Burn).   *Rule: stay on the bank of the stream (you'll cross it twice) until you've passed a double-decker bridge.*   (Lower deck = 1611, upper = 1788.)   Soon, leave the stream by turning *right*, up steps.   Join main park roadway (toilets 100m to right) but you can go left up more steps to visit alleged ruin of King Malcolm Canmore's and his Queen Margaret's Tower.   Continue   past   Tower   up   to   Park   gate   and Dunfermline Abbey.   (Historic Scotland: summer closing 6 pm; winter 4 pm.)

Dunfermline Abbey

To explore: Abbot House, Abbey, Palace, and Carnegie Museum are good value.   So is the (free) access to St Margaret's Cave, daily 11 am to 4 pm in spring and summer: go up "Kirkgate" from Abbey, cross to "Bruce Street" and find pedestrian access, on left, to a car park.   There, up to your right, is the cave entrance building.

SECTION 4

DUNFERMLINE (Abbey)
TO KINGSEAT (Hotel): 6km (4 miles)

This short section takes us out of Dunfermline via its pedestrianised High Street and a disused rail line until, turning towards Kingseathill – which we cross – we make our way to Townhill Country Park and on to the village of Kingseat.

Let's Walk! Use the Map.

(1)   Stand on the roadway where we emerged from Pittencreiff Park, at the end of Section 3. With Park gates on your left and Abbey on your right, proceed uphill.   Turn second right into the pedestrianised High Street.   At the end of the pedestrian zone, continue in the same direction *making sure you are on the right hand side of the road.* You'll pass Baptist and Episcopal churches (both on right).   Then: **ATTENTION PLEASE**, enter an opening on the right at a "Museum" sign but continue parallel to the road (but at a higher level).   Beyond Carnegie Hall, you come down to a path T-junction where you turn right (away from a traffic roundabout).   Then turn left to cross a footbridge over a dual carriageway.   Turn left and go down to cross the wide road in front of you, making use of the traffic signals by the roundabout.   On the far side, turn right – passing a house – to cross a side road at more traffic signals.   On the far side, turn left.   Then bear right, away from the road and turn right in front of a lock up.   Go ahead (pedestrian/cycle sign) and seek out a small roundabout about half way along the car park you have entered.

(2)   From this roundabout, go over to the road which runs along the far side of the car park (NT 098878).   Turn right on the road and, soon, take the cycle/footway (sign "Kinross") which runs along the line of an old railway and passes a football ground (right) and large cemetery (left).   Go on, through a gate and down, under a bridge.   **STOP UNDER THE BRIDGE.**   When I say 'Go', walk on for about 5 minutes – ignoring gaps in the cemetery hedge – while you count 13 lamp posts.   'Go!'

(3)   Now you'll find official gates on *both* sides of the path.   Turn *left* here, then, ignoring a junction (right), walk uphill (laurel bushes on left) and passing a play area (right). At a road, cross and go right – still going up.   At a T-junction (end of "Craigston Drive"), turn left.   In a few metres, opposite a bus stop (*right*), turn right up concrete steps.   The Way goes over the brow of a hill and down to a road which you cross (shops on left).   Continue on the same straight line, uphill.   Up at the next road, turn left and, almost immediately, right to take the continuing path up behind a letter box, as you enjoy the views.   Cross a main road carefully to follow down the still continuing (but now unsurfaced) path.   Go straight ahead, where National Cycle Route No 1 crosses the Way, and head towards houses.   At a T-junction with a surfaced road, turn right.   Cross mouth of "Woodlands Grove" (left) and turn next left into "Forest Place".

(4)   Just over a rise, turn right into "Townhill Country Park", going through a kissing gate into woodland.   Fork right, soon gaining views over parts of Dunfermline and the River Forth to the Pentland Hills in the distance.   After topping a gentle rise, the main path turns sharp left (and you ignore a lesser path going ahead).   Near the top of Townhill, you pass a fenced-in underground reservoir.   Bear gently left on the track leading away from the gated compound.   Soon, you ignore a junction on your left but, some 50m from the compound you come to a clear side path (right).   *Turn right, here,* soon passing under electricity cables.   This leads to a car-parking and turning area.   *Turn right here, also,* through a kissing gate to another footpath which meanders gently. Presently, you *take a left fork.*   Soon *take a second left fork,* leading to a path where you bear right to follow electricity poles down a hollow.

At the start of farmland, go through a gap in the fence [gate needed, 2009] to walk along a farm track.   At a track T-junction, turn left towards houses at Muircockhall.   Main track curves right then left (keeping houses on your left).

(5)   At crest, **turn right** in front of a cottage (which you also keep on your left) to follow a grassy wheel track: Hill of Beath, ahead.   (You may have to skirt right of a wet area, taking care to keep off crops.)   Resume your *exactly original*

straight line, with fences on both sides of you and soon with houses over the right hand fence. [If path is very overgrown you can dodge over the left hand fence]. The path channels you into the "closed" end of a cul-de-sac, "Frew Place", which leads into the main road through Kingseat. Turn left and Section 4 ends in a few metres at the hotel: "Half Way House". Most guests apparently come on wheels so, if you're going in, you'll find the front door in the car park, round the back. (I'm being a little unfair: there is also a street door – though a tad less dramatic.)

By the way, (as indeed we are), "Half Way House" is reputedly half way from Dunfermline to Kelty *by road*. Strangely enough, within a very few kilometres, and before we cross to the north side of the B 914 (see next section's map), *we* shall be half way to St Andrews!

Oh, if you can't resist climbing the 240m Hill of Beath: fork right into "Cuddyhouse Road" just beyond the hotel. Beyond the end of the houses, take the track on the right. Cross motorway and take stile on left. Go ahead, with hill on right, till finding a suitable point to strike upwards.

SECTION 5

KINGSEAT (Hotel) TO KELTYBRIDGE:
Present Route 10km (6 miles)
Future Route 8km (4½ miles)

As noted in 'Features of the Walk', Section 5, on page 24, the scenery is being moved around, literally! The map, opposite, shows the **Present Route** and indicates that the landscaped Fife Earth Project will replace the opencast mine. However, Scottish Coal are applying (2010) for planning permission to move the mining area southwards – involving the draining of Loch Fitty and closing the path shown. (So local people tell me.) We cannot yet map the **Future Route**, but the good news is, it will be 2km (about 1 mile) shorter – running near the M 90 – and we can use this text to guide us on out way. We can rely on Fife Council to ensure pedestrian signs indicate "Kelty".

Let's Walk! Use the Map.
   (6)   Continue on the road through Kingseat. At the end of the roadside footway, turn left down tarmac lane towards Loch Fitty. *[If, at the top of this lane, or on the way down, you see a "Kelty" sign, then the **Future Route** has arrived – see below, page 59.]*

   Present Route (map):   Cross Loch Fitty causeway, then turn left to cross the footbridge over the outflow, and follow the path. Beyond a gate (see map) and two ponds, you have to turn left to cross a ditch; then *immediately turn right to go parallel to the ditch.* Later, the path passes a third pond. Go ahead between two further ponds (map). Ignore junction (right). Pass a picnic table, then curve right to pass a landscape interpretation board. At next junction, turn left and head uphill. Through gate and *curve left* at junction. **NOW**, at successive junctions, curve right on main path. Pass (right) a limestone quarry interpretation board (NT 109929). Ignore turnings until main path goes through a gate and leads on, into a car park.

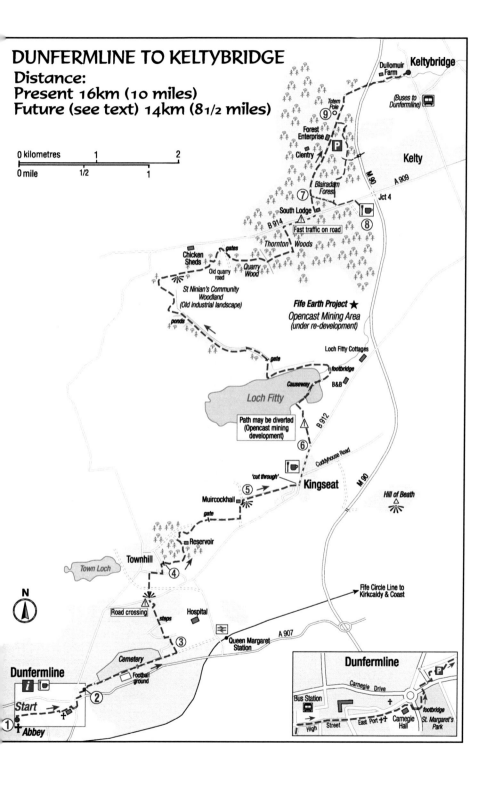

DUNFERMLINE TO KELTYBRIDGE

Distance:
Present 16km (10 miles)
Future (see text) 14km (8½ miles)

0 kilometres 1 2
0 mile 1/2 1

Keltybridge
Dullomuir Farm
(Buses to Dunfermline)
Totem Pole
⑨
Forest Enterprise
Clentry
Kelty
A 909
M 90
Blairadam Forest
Jct 4
⑦
South Lodge
Fast traffic on road
B 914
⑧
Thornton Woods
Chicken Sheds
gates
Old quarry road
Quarry Wood
St Ninian's Community Woodland
(Old industrial landscape)

Fife Earth Project ★
Opencast Mining Area
(under re-development)

ponds
gate
Loch Fitty Cottages
footbridge
B&B
Causeway
Loch Fitty
B 912
Path may be diverted
(Opencast mining development)
⑥
Cuddyhouse Road
'cut through'
Kingseat
Muircockhall
⑤
gate
Hill of Beath
M 90
Reservoir
Town Loch
Townhill
④
Fife Circle Line to Kirkcaldy & Coast
Road crossing
Hospital
steps
③
Queen Margaret Station
A 907

N

Cemetery
Football ground
Dunfermline
②
Start
①
Abbey

Dunfermline
Carnegie Drive
Bus Station
footbridge
St. Margaret's Park
High Street
East Port
Carnegie Hall

From the car park, turn right to enter a further asphalt-surfaced area. Bear left through a large gate to "Quarry Wood". At a fork, bear left on grassy path. **ATTENTION; Path curves right. At its very closest point to Thornton Wood (NT 121931) turn left – lightly trodden – to cross ditch and go through flap in fence into Thornton Wood.** Cross a ditch inside, on a very small bridge, and walk, via planting furrows, to an overgrown track. At track junction, turn left to B 914 road and there turn right. Turn left, off B 914, at "South Lodge" into woodland.

(7) 250m from the road, you have a choice: Either: turn right to return to the road where you'll soon find Baxters Restaurant (right) (8). Or: continue straight ahead on estate road, passing forestry offices then (9) a totem pole (left). Go straight on down to foot of hill where you go right at a junction, under the M 90, to Keltybridge. [Dunfermline buses, 350m to right].

Future Route (not mapped): If, and when, further mining closes the Loch Fitty path, signs "Kelty" will tell you about it. We can expect Scottish Coal and Fife Council to have slightly different opinions. Scottish Coal will want us to march straight on down the B 912 road from Kingseat (verge but no footway) – passing Lassodie War Memorial – to a new path bearing left (look for "Kelty" sign, somewhere *between* "Lochfitty Cottage" B&B and the *next* group of cottages which has a street sign "Loch Fitty Cottages". This will lead you northwards, parallel to the M 90, skirting the east side of the new landscaping, to the B 914 road (with Baxters on your right). Fife Council will doubtless prefer a (safer?) off-road path parallel to the B 912 road. Just follow signs. [If you find a clear opportunity – which should be available in the course of time – to dodge left to visit the new landscaping (see below), I would recommend this. The main exit from the landscaping will be to the north, near to Baxters Restaurant.]

(8) From Baxters Restaurant: Cross the B 914, turn left along the footway and, soon, turn right into surfaced estate road. Just past the car-parking area here, turn right onto a footpath. This meanders (ignore a junction on left) till you

59

come down to, and go straight across, a cross path.   Go down
to, and cross, a footbridge; then bear right, uphill.

(9)   Beyond a vehicle barrier, turn right on a track –
passing a totem pole (left) – and going straight on down to the
foot of the hill where you go right at a junction, under the M
90, to Keltybridge.   [Bus stop for Dunfermline is 350m to
right, along the road.]

Loch Fitty causeway – to disappear?

The landscaping of Fife Earth Project is to feature four
large geometric mounds, or hills, each to represent a continent
which Scotland has influenced – discuss. Nestling amongst
them we should find 'Scot Loch', a small loch which will be
shaped like Scotland and is to be filled, initially, with water
pumped from Loch Fitty.   We should be able to view all this
from a path rising uphill, northwards, on the east side of a
further larger, loch which is to have an *island* shaped like
Scotland.

SECTION 6: PREAMBLE

A NOTE ABOUT THE R.S.P.B. VANE FARM NATURE RESERVE

Vane Farm Nature Reserve is run by the Royal Society for the Protection of Birds, of which I am a member. The area is private and one does not have the 'right to roam' under Scottish Access legislation. However, the R.S.P.B. welcomes walkers and encourages them to use its coffee shop. Let us, for a moment, consider walkers on The Saint Andrew's Way from the Society's point of view. The very existence of the Society is to support bird life (and Vane Farm borders Loch Leven – itself a National Nature reserve) but the Society extends its remit to the support of the natural environment, and – by stretching a point – it includes sympathetically minded walkers through that environment: us! If you have a dog: keep it under close control (this usually means a lead) and keep it outside the farm coffee shop. If you are in doubt, the route notes help you avoid Vane Farm. I think it behoves us to make a purchase in the centre's shop or coffee shop by way of our 'thank you'. You may even consider the benefits of membership!

Loch Leven from Vane Hill

61

SECTION 6

KELTYBRIDGE
TO VANE FARM: 8km (5 miles)

In the previous section, we sneaked out of Fife: the Kelty
Burn is the boundary.   We soon re-enter Fife to walk over
Harran Hill and the eastern shoulder of Benarty Hill.   We
leave Fife again to enter Vane Farm Nature Reserve which is
in Perth and Kinross: but we find ourselves so completely
knocked out by the views over Loch Leven that we don't give
county boundaries another thought.   Pssst!   You won't re-
enter Fife again till Section 8!

Let's Walk! Use the Map.
    (1)   Where you emerged onto the public road in
Keltybridge, turn left and immediately right at an unsigned
(2009) public right of way which tries to disguise itself as a
vehicle driveway with two rows of concrete slabs.   *Beyond*
the last house, go through the gate and follow round the right
edge of a field.   Another gate takes you into a meadow which
leads you to a kissing gate at the B 966 – the former Great
North Road – where you cross and turn left.   In 250m, turn
right into a "cul-de-sac" leading towards Loch Ore Meadows
Country Park.   Beyond some houses and after re-entering Fife
(no sign) and an 800m (½ mile) straight, go round a left curve.
    (2)   Turn left through a gate (sign "Harran Hill").   Your
uphill track offers views of Loch Ore (right).   At a bench
(left) the track curves left and steepens, before levelling off.
Near the opposite side of Harran Hill, your track swings right
(ignoring a grassy left fork) but soon **curves left down to a
gate**.   Go through and turn left.
    (3)   Cross public road and go up steps opposite (sign
"Benarty").   Despite fewer than two hundred steps, you may
choose to stop for a breather, perhaps catching a further view
of Loch Ore – a former coal mining area – with a concrete
monument representing coal pit winding gear.   New
Zealanders call these things "poppet heads".   (Just thought
you'd like to know!)   At the top: a forest track and a well-
placed bench.   Turn right, downhill on the track: noting

Largo Law (hill) in the distance.   At a forest track junction, fork left, er, uphill.   Presently, you'll see a fence and stone dyke crossing your way in front of you.

(4)   Do **NOT** go round the left-hand hairpin bend here. Instead: go ahead to the fence.   **Go left for the few metres up to its** *extreme left hand end* **and turn right to cross the fence (watch: barbed wire) to a field which, initially, is only about 2m wide!**   Walk along the *left* edge of the field (no visible path in 2009) with forest on left.   Keep bearing left, sticking to the fence and woodland on your left.   *Soon after the forest ends* (at NT 164983), you can cross the fence on your left.   **Do so!**   Also cross the parallel ancient ruined wall and carry on down, past four pine trees – noting how I am leading you past a muddy slippery area at a spring.   Once you are down in the field below, head for the **PROMINENT** electricity pylon standing in rough moorland ahead.   [If you can't see the pylon for mist, simply skirt round inside the left edge of this lower field.]   As you make your way towards the pylon, you will note it stands amidst regenerating plant growth – it's in Vane Farm Nature Reserve!

(5)   As you pass the pylon you should, *just before the eastern boundary of the reserve,* **turn left to step over the fence you have been following** and out of Fife.   [Oh, for a gate (2009)!]   Follow a trodden way (fence on your right and Loch Leven ahead) for 300m to Vane Farm's viewpoint on Vane Hill.   [If you have decided to avoid Vane Farm, go down to the loch *outside* that eastern boundary fence.   Part of the descent is very steep but gates let you cross the road below.   Take care: fast traffic!]   From the benches and cairn at the viewpoint, continue **towards** Loch Leven, by going down the steeply stepped footpath (take care!) which soon curves left.   At a path junction, join the "Birchwood Loop" by turning **right** and following the path down to a grassy picnic area and the R.S.P.B Visitor Centre with its café, shop, and toilets.

KELTYBRIDGE to SCOTLANDWELL
Distance: 13km (8 miles)

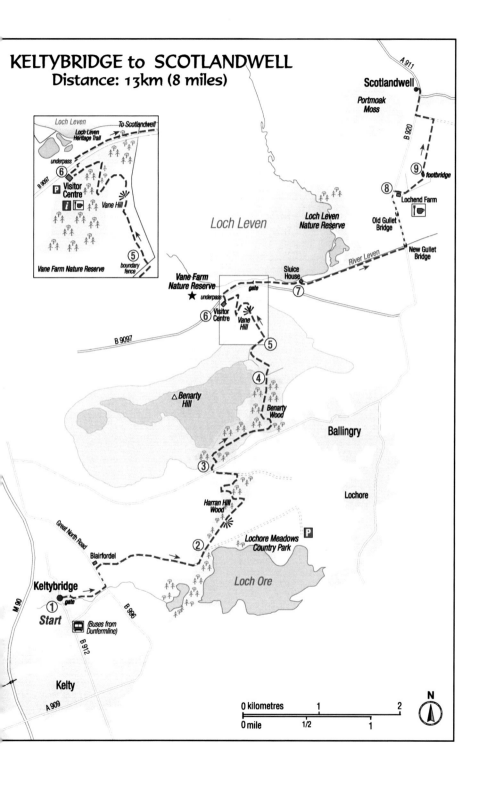

Loch Leven

To Scotlandwell

Loch Leven Heritage Trail

underspass

Visitor Centre

Vane Hill

Vane Farm Nature Reserve

boundary fence

Loch Leven Nature Reserve

Loch Leven

Scotlandwell

Portmoak Moss

footbridge

Lochend Farm

Old Gullet Bridge

New Gullet Bridge

River Leven

Sluice House

Vane Farm Nature Reserve

underpass

gate

Visitor Centre

Vane Hill

B 9097

Benarty Hill

Benarty Wood

Ballingry

Lochore

Harran Hill Wood

Lochore Meadows Country Park

Loch Ore

Great North Road

Blairfordel

Keltybridge

Start

gate

(Buses from Dunfermline)

Kelty

M 90

B 996

B 912

A 909

A 911

B 920

0 kilometres   1   2

0 mile   1/2   1

N

SECTION 7

VANE FARM
TO SCOTLANDWELL: 5km (3 miles)

This is the shortest section of the Way, though a compass may
come in handy! Our gratitude goes to the county of Perth and
Kinross who, with the blessing of the R.S.P.B., formed the
Loch Leven Heritage Trail which leads us from Vane Farm;
and also to the proprietors of Lochend Farm who welcome
walkers and run an excellent farm shop/café and enable us to
dodge most of the public road into Scotlandwell.   Not only is
this the shortest section, it is also the flattest; and is the only
section, north of the Forth, which is wholly outwith Fife.

Let's Walk!   Use the Map.
   (6)   To continue your walk from the Visitor Centre:
stand, facing Loch Leven, and with your back to the Centre.
Move ahead and turn right, so that the B 9097 road is on your
left.   Soon, by a totem pole which is easily mistaken for a
telegraph pole, you turn left, down steps through a pedestrian
subway under the road.   Then, turn right to follow the Loch
Leven Heritage Trail.   A gate marks your departure from the
R.S.P.B. territory and you move nearer the loch.   **Ignore a
right turn** and soon you pass a sandy beach and then the
sluice house where the river flows out of the loch.
   (7)   Now, walk in a *straight line* for 1km (¾ mile), *keeping*
the river on your left and **ignoring** a tempting footbridge
which crosses it.   At the main B 920 road, turn left, crossing
New Gullet Bridge.   The man-made river channel runs ruler
straight for 5km (3 miles) and drains the local farm land (to a
certain extent, see below!)   The river has also lowered the
level of Loch Leven, which was appreciably higher when
Mary Queen of Scots was imprisoned for a year on Castle
Island.   Next, you cross Old Gullet Bridge and pass the
Scottish Gliding Centre (left) as you round the curve with
care.
   (8)   Turn right at Lochend Farm Shop.   (Squeeze past the
gate with the 'cart wheels').   Farm and shop are run by the
most delightful and helpful couple: Michael and Helen.

65

Trouble is, Michael has ploughed and planted across a strip which he was "keeping free for walkers" to Scotlandwell. *I shall carefully describe the point you are to aim for from the shop.* It is a footbridge at NO 186707 across a drainage ditch which bounds part of the north side of Michael's large field located north of the shop. It is 330m due east of "Red House" (marked on OS 1:50,000 and 1:25,000 scale maps). *But you can not see it from the shop!* If the field is harvested and you have a compass: walk on a magnetic bearing of 53 degrees (2009) to the bridge. If you have no compass or GPS, ask the shop staff for their help. If all else fails, walk *just inside the field edge*, first adjacent to the road, then turn right at "Red House", along the north edge of the field to the bridge.

(9) From the bridge, it's easy! Go north along a grassy strip by the left edge of the next field. You are heading towards the golf ball tower on the top of Munduff Hill. The Way becomes more track-like as you continue in a straight line. Only when you are forced to turn at a T-junction, should you go left to the road. Turn right on the road and enter Scotlandwell. Section 7 ends at the well, itself, which is signposted (left), opposite "Leslie Road".

Scotlandwell: the Well

66

SECTION 8

SCOTLANDWELL
TO FALKLAND (PALACE):   14km (8½ miles)

"Today's walk," averred one of our walkers, "really gives the St. Andrew's Way its teeth".   Certainly the stretch up Munduff Hill is breathtaking.   Either I refer to the view over Loch Leven or the upward gradient – *both,* probably!   We cross the Lomond Hills plateau, passing Harperleas and Ballo Reservoirs.   [Keen hill-climbers may readily conquer West and East Lomonds.   You would head for West Lomond from the west end of Harperleas Reservoir (map); then visit East Lomond before descending to Falkland: but you'd miss Maspie Den!]   The St. Andrew's Way goes from Ballo to Craigmead Car Park and down Maspie Den, passing *behind* the Yad Waterfall – a hidden gem – to the regularly flower-bedecked Falkland and its Palace.

Let's Walk!   Use the Map.
   (1)   On leaving the Well, turn left on the main road, passing the "Well Country Inn" (right).   50m before 40 mph signs, turn right "Footpath to Bishop Hill".   Where the path turns left and levels off, <u>PAY ATTENTION</u>!   In 2 minutes (when you're above a *shallow* valley), **fork right** onto a *narrow uphill path*, **very soon turning right** on a *trodden* higher path.   (Map reveals you've just short circuited the first of two hair-pin bends.)   This, rather overgrown, track heads up to the second hairpin bend where you **turn sharp left** and pass a seat (or sit on it).   Keep to main path till kissing gate (NO 186027) leads you onto moor.   [In *very* poor visibility, you *could* follow the wall to the right, round the edge of the moor and right up the hill; but it requires a short scramble.]   Otherwise, ahead from gate: in a minute, **fork right** to a rocky outcrop above you.   Path aims to right of old spoil heap and curves left *behind it* to pass old quarry (dry stone walls) on your right.   Follow the steep path up, keeping left of, and away from the top of, a small cliff.

67

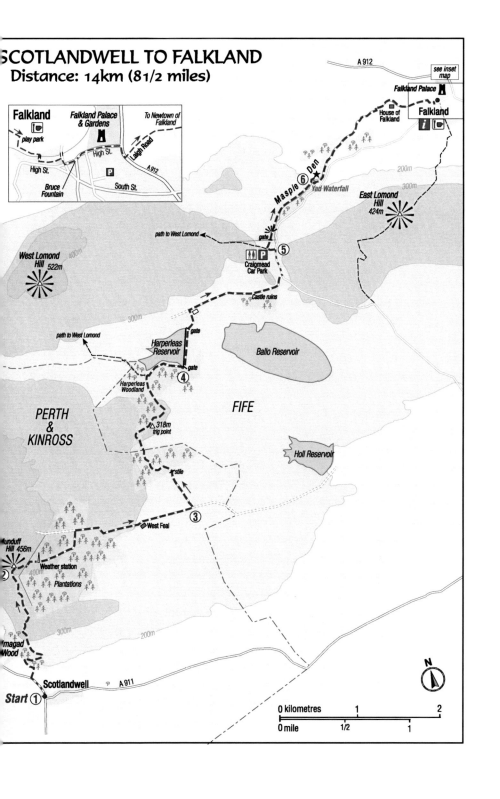

SCOTLANDWELL TO FALKLAND
Distance: 14km (8½ miles)

A 912

see inset map

Falkland Palace

Falkland

Falkland

play park

Falkland Palace & Gardens

To Newtown of Falkland

High St.

Leigh Road

High St.

A 912

P

South St.

Bruce Fountain

House of Falkland

i

200m

300m

Maspie Den

6

Yad Waterfall

East Lomond Hill 424m

path to West Lomond

gate

5

Craigmead Car Park

P

West Lomond Hill 522m

400m

300m

Castle ruins

Ballo Reservoir

gate

Harperleas Reservoir

gate

4

Harperleas Woodland

318m trig point

FIFE

PERTH & KINROSS

Holl Reservoir

stile

3

West Feal

unduff Hill 456m

Weather station

Plantations

2

400m

300m

200m

magad Wood

Scotlandwell

A 911

Start 1

N

0 kilometres   1   2

0 mile   1/2   1

On the grass above the cliff, fork right *uphill*, to follow grassy narrow path. As the summit of Munduff Hill comes into view, your path heads left of it into a shallow valley where you bear right (indistinct path), towards a saddle and thence to summit cairn.

(2)   From the cairn, make your way across the stone dyke to the adjacent wood. With the wood on your right, find – just a few metres down – a narrow trodden way, where you turn right through the trees, to a meteorological station (the golf ball thing). Here a vehicle track takes you down to a cross track (map) where you turn right, downhill, to pass West Feal.

(3)   About ½ km (500 yards) beyond West Feal, turn left at "Harperleas" sign. A stile (map) leads into woodland which is often wet underfoot. Another stile, where a grassy path crosses the way, leads you on a meandering route passing a nearby trig point (right) and down to a main track. Turn right, skirting Harperleas Reservoir – seen through trees (left).

(4)   At end of reservoir, turn left through gate (map) to cross dam. At far end, another gate takes you up a grassy path to a wheel track. Turn right, passing Castle ruins (map). At public road, go left to Craigmead Car Park.

(5)   From Craigmead's toilet block, walk further from the road to the back right hand corner of the car park and take footpath signed "West Lomond". Go through a gate and *ahead* and slightly downhill, crossing a vehicle track at another gate and entering forest. Soon, **a further gate** leads down into a valley through regenerating woodland (2009). At a path junction, **turn left**, soon to cross a footbridge and continuing generally downhill with a wall (left) bounding your woodland. Ignore side turnings and come to *a further gate*. **Then, in about 50m, ignore the first small footpath which doubles back to your right.**

(6)   **In a further 20 or 30m take the _next_ (i.e. second) small footpath which doubles back to your right.** This takes you down to pass *behind* Maspie Den's secret waterfall! 5 or 10 minutes downstream from the waterfall, having crossed the stream several times, at a path junction on the left bank, **fork right, down** to cross another bridge. Soon you cross back to the left bank where a vehicle bridge goes over

your head! Next surprise: your main path down the left bank enters a tunnel. This is cunningly curved so that light appears ahead just when you were panicking in the dark. Stay on the left bank until, below a house (right), you cross a footbridge to the right bank. Next, *fork up to your right* but stay with the valley. At surfaced road, turn right. At crossroads, turn left to cross bridge: then turn right. Follow main path, downstream. Ignore a path junction (right; which leads down to stables – estate offices – and to a car park). However, you must take the *next* path junction to the right, which is rather informal but ramps down to a play area by the burn. Go through the play area past a house (left) which makes our path look like its front garden. After the next house (right), turn sharp right across a footbridge onto a path leading round to village streets. Go uphill with "Stag Inn" on your left and turn left at T-junction to Falkland Palace (National Trust for Scotland).

The Square, Falkland

SECTION 9

FALKLAND
TO CERES: 21km (13 miles)

Today, we wander through a series of small communities in, and beyond, the River Eden plain, or the Howe of Fife – as they call it – an Anglicised version of Gaelic 'haugh', meaning low-lying land by a river.   We touch upon Newton of Falkland;   and   pass   through   Kingskettle,   Balmalcolm, Kettlehill, Burnturk, Chance Inn, and Craigrothie.   As you cross the flat bit, you may ponder (I use the word deliberately) on the effects of heavy rain.   Should you have brought your wellingtons?   In Kingskettle, a sign "Shorehead" suggests safety here!   The second half of the Section takes us up towards Down Law and along higher ground, finally to enter Ceres along a sample section of the ancient Bishop's Road which conducted pilgrims from Kennoway to St Andrews.

Let's Walk!   Use the Map.
  (1)   On coming out the gate of Falkland Palace, turn left and – on reaching the main road – turn right.   In a few metres, turn left at a sign "Laigh Road to Newton of Falkland" to enter a lane which soon becomes a grassy path.   Stay with the path for 1km (½ mile), crossing one lane, but emerging on a surfaced road (small park, left).   Turn left, cross a bridge, and road soon bends right.   At end of straight, *do NOT curve left* because our Way goes *straight on* along a grassy path leading into woodland.   At a surfaced, estate, road, (NO 277080) turn right.   In 1km, at cross roads, turn left.
  (2)   *After* passing "Easter Lathrisk House" (on right), you turn right into surfaced farm road at sign "Easter Lathrisk Farm: Private Road".   Walk through, respecting farm operations.   At next, main, road – the A 92 trunk road – *cross with great care* – onto a track directly opposite.   Note: you are following overhead power cables.   Where these change direction slightly, turn right to cross a bridge and aim straight for the left end of a copse.   (That section has, in the past, been found to have been ploughed.)

71

FALKLAND TO CERES
Distance: 21km (13 miles)

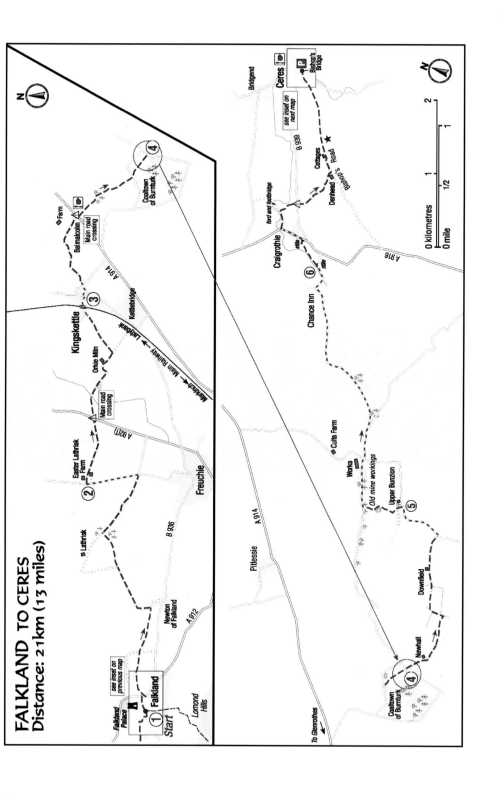

After a pond (right), go past farm buildings (keeping them on your left).   150m beyond the buildings, at next track junction, *turn left* to Kingskettle, where you pass (or enter) the "Station Inn".   Walk under railway bridge and turn right into "Church Wynd".   At main road, turn left, and then turn right into "Crown Square".   At far end – on the left – take short alley to another road.   Turn left to pass shop and post office.

(3)   At main road, cross.   Go round churchyard to your right (keeping it on your left) to enter side road "Shorehead". Follow this to Balmalcolm.   Cross the main A 914 with *care*. "Muddy Boots" restaurant is to your   left, and is recommended,   Otherwise, turn right and, almost immediately, left, at sign "Public right of way to Kettlehill and Burnturk".   Our path goes almost straight up, making partial use of an ancient sunken lane and emerging at a kissing gate to pass farm buildings and continue as a surfaced lane.   Cross a road and continue on a footpath (sign "Putting Green").   Path curves left and turns right to pass the putting green and clubhouse (right).

(4)   At next road, cross straight over and walk up surfaced drive, respecting any livestock (wood on right).   At end of lane, move right (bridge over ditch) and take high gate ahead, closing it behind you.   Continue on same line on farm track which soon bends past cottages, so that you are aiming towards a hill with radio masts.   At the upper edge of a field (old tree, 2009), the Way turns sharp left along the field edge then curves right, passing houses.   At road, turn left.   Walk along road for 800m (½ mile).

(5)   Turn left on farm track by a small wood.   At track junction, go straight ahead.   Now, curve left to field gate. Enter and go down and round right hand side.   Exit through gate (which is on the original line of the ancient track) at bottom right hand corner of field.   Take path downwards, soon curving left past a pond; but turn right into wood at NO 347086 and follow path to road.   [Note: the track between the roads was originally straight(ish).]   Turn right along road. Go straight ahead at cross roads (sign "Chance Inn 1½") and at next junction, fork left (*two* signs "Chance Inn 1½" and "Chance Inn 1¼").   Down to your left, you may see evidence

of the old coal railway along the valley side. In Chance Inn, turn right at road junction (sign "Craigrothie ¾").

(6) *Just before the road rises uphill,* beside an electricity pole and a yellow salt bin (left), look for an arrow pointing to a stile on the left. (Hint: the arrow is facing walkers coming *down* the hill.) Cross the stile and follow path, then cross a second stile. Follow faint path (fence and stream on left). Soon, cross a third stile ahead and skirt round to right of low-lying area (probably fenced off). Bear right, diagonally up field, towards the first house on the A 916 road. Cross the wall at an old stile in the field corner and where you'll see a bus stop on the road; but watch out for the barbed wire. This was the miners' way to work. Turn left down road (primary school and an inn, both on left). Before a bridge, turn right down "Old Mill Road". Some 80m after the footway ends, the road forks. I suggest you go *both* ways!

First: Take left fork for 140m to view ford and pedestrian bridge.

Secondly: Return. Take right fork. Go round "Old Mill Cottage" (left) and past ruinous dovecote (right), Before "The Old Mill", itself, fork right up narrow path. Cross B 939 road carefully into "Denhead" road, opposite. Just past the farm, we turn left and we're on Bishop's Road where Archbishop Sharp travelled on the night he was murdered in 1679. At Ceres, cross road to the car park. Section 9 ends at the 17th century bridge over the burn. See information boards. Toilets are on your left.

SECTION 10

CERES
TO ST ANDREWS: 16km (10 miles)

The astute navigator of Section 10 will spot that we make use of at least two ancient routes into town.   First, we bear uphill so we don't have to hack through vegetation along the Ceres Burn, but we change to the route via Kininmonth because it aims more directly at St Andrews.   If you've spotted that the ending of Kininmonth means 'hill', you're correct!   It is the last ascent of the Way.   Once up, we maintain height for a while, then our spirits slowly rise as our altitude slowly lowers on our way down to ancient Kinrymont.   You may see references to *'Kilrymont'*.   Are the townsfolk confused?   Why is the present name of the town in the plural?   In any event, you will enjoy your stroll down the Lade Braes Walk into *St Andrew's!*

Let's Walk!   Use the Map.
    (1)   Starting back in Ceres car park, cross the old stone arch bridge.   Turn left.   Where the lane widens, at Fife Folk Museum, turn sharp right on narrow road past cottages and play area.   At two-lane 'main' road, turn half left and cross to walk past a row of houses (right) with a vehicle parking/turning area (left).   Turn right along "School Hill" (flat!).   At end, go through gate at right hand side of end house, where a sign "Callange" is pointing (2009) in a rather confusing direction.   Continue up field edge (fence on right) to join a track and maintain the same direction.   Avoid side turnings until, at top of rise, bear left and go through gate into wood.   At end of wood, go through field gate ahead (by water tank/bath).   [If you find it *so* muddy here that even the cattle are standing to one side, try choosing a route parallel to the one about to be described – but on the right hand side of the fence.]   Beyond the tank, follow right edge of field.   Pass two ancient beech trees to fence corner in a further 30m.   Cross stile [noting how those diverted by mud can rejoin here] and

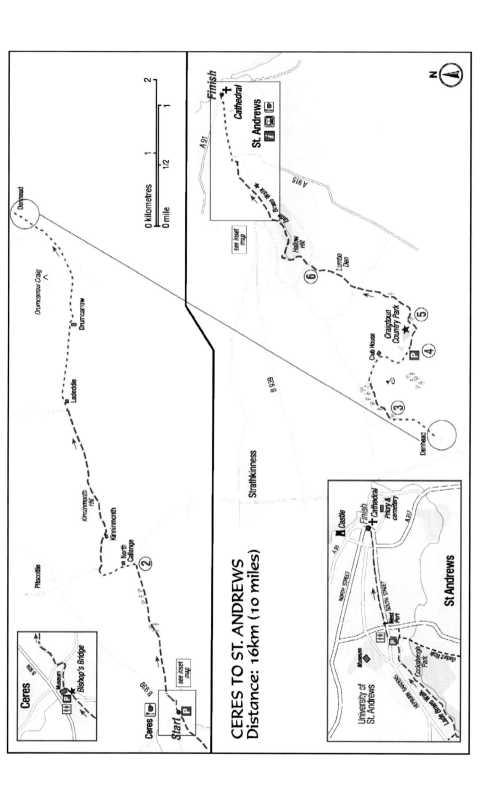

CERES TO ST. ANDREWS
Distance: 16km (10 miles)

continue, still in the same direction, ignoring side turnings, until you come to main road where you **STOP!**

(2) While stationary, note plaque (right) about Mr Lunardi's aerial voyage. Also note Kininmonth Hill ahead (slightly left). Turn left down road. *(Traffic!)* At foot, go round right hand bend, and turn right to "Kininmonth" (sign "Right of Way to Laddedie 2.5km"). Up the hill; over the top; and soon join a surfaced road. Keep ahead, same direction. In 2km (1¼ miles), bear left on main road – still maintaining direction. Over a crest and down at next junction, fork right to another Denhead – and still maintaining your direction. After Denhead's last house, the road curves left and is then *straight*.

(3) Some 200m along this straight, **turn right through a one metre gap in the wall (at NO 470143) where a finger post sign says "St Andrews". IMPORTANT: The path we want** *turns left behind the wall to go parallel to the road.* It does, in fact, keep the golf course on your right. *Stay on main path* through woodland. Eventually, go *straight* across a tarmac path and on to a gate, giving access to a road, where you turn right.   Stay on road past car park (right) and golf club house (left) towards Craigton Country Park. (It's worth a visit, given the time and the cash.)

(4) You'll pass a car park and bus park for the Country Park. Where the road reaches *the far end of the car park* (but without turning towards the country park entrance) go through gate straight ahead to follow the path – which moves gently left – soon to skirt the Country Park, keeping it on your immediate left.

(5) Simply follow this path till you come to a finger post sign. Turn right ("St Andrews") between bushes. Soon, at a cross path by a wooden pole (number "25")   which supports power cables, bear left on the main path. Use gates to cross a narrow road and keep on down the valley – strolling through the trees.

Cross a public road via gates (house on right) and take path *ahead*, by stream. **In about 30m,** *fork right* to cross stream on a plank bridge.   In a few more metres, fork right again, upwards. Our path does follow the stream, but near the top of the right slope of the valley. Eventually, we come back down to re-cross the stream on a similar plank bridge. [Crossing the stream twice wasn't strictly necessary, but I prefer the right!]

(6)   Bear right and go downstream on a gravel path. Ignore side turnings. When you cross the next road, find the continuing path to the left of the bus shelter. Return to the main path if you visit the dovecote. At next path junction, turn left to "Town Centre" passing a pond and an old mill. At the foot of a slope, cross the bridge (sign). Then turn right to pass a metal cycle barrier.

Path opens out at a grass area. Bear right to follow stream, but *don't cross bridge* (to Hallow Hill). Soon, path goes round far gable end of pan-tiled cottages and down past more metal barriers. Again: don't cross bridge. Follow main path. You pass a play area, Cockshaugh Park, and emerge to cross the end of a street. Straight ahead here – past more metal barriers – into narrow lane leading through houses. At junction of lanes, turn right. At cross path, "Viaduct Walk", turn left and go through car park.

On the street, *turn right* (Argyle Street). It's better to walk on the *left* side. Cross City Road at traffic island. Go through West Port's old town wall arches into South Street. You pass the ruins of the Blackfriars' chapel (right). At the far end of the street, turn left. The Cathedral and the end of the Saint Andrew's Way are on your right.

Do take time to explore the Cathedral and to climb St Rule's tower (at the far end). You should also visit the nearby Castle, with its exciting 'mine and counter-mine', where defenders dug a tunnel outwards and intercepted attackers tunnelling in! There are so many things to see and do in academic, cosmopolitan, St Andrews. What a pity we forgot to carry our golf clubs with us! Thank you for coming out to play; it was fun, don't you think? If you enjoyed yourselves, please tell others. And we should *all* be told about the first intrepid pilgrim who *does* carry a full set of golf clubs from Edinburgh!

Saint Andrew's Cathedral

I promised in Part I to say more about 'other bits' of St Andrew. Some of his relics found their way to Rome from Patras, but most went to Constantinople on the Roman Emperor Constantine's orders; and, very much later, to Amalfi, Italy to keep them safe from French Crusaders. If you visit Saint Mary's RC Cathedral, Edinburgh (750m from the *start* of the Way), you can see a piece of shoulder bone (Amalfi) and a small piece of skull (Rome). A third relic is *here*, in St Andrews – in St James RC Church, The Scores. So: if you're curious . . . But don't let me raise your hopes – it is not on show.

Public Transport Information

supplied by Barry Cross

Fife and Edinburgh are well served by public transport so it is simple to walk The Way in sections of one, two or more days at a time.

Train
First Scotrail services link Edinburgh (Waverley and Haymarket Stations) with Fife. There are
A number of stations convenient for the Way;

Edinburgh Waverley
Edinburgh Haymarket
Dalmeny *(1km from The Way at Queensferry)*
North Queensferry
Inverkeithing
Rosyth
Dunfermline Town
Dunfermline St Margarets
Ladybank *(1km from The Way at Kingskettle)*
Cupar *(3km from The Way at Ceres)*
Leuchars**

**   There is a frequent bus service between St Andrews and Leuchars railway station with a journey time of about 10 minutes. You can buy through bus/train tickets at all stations on the rail network or at St Andrews bus station.

Bus – see next page.

Bus

Frequent Stagecoach bus services link Edinburgh with Fife and serve many of the communities through which The Way passes. The most useful are;

Service	Route	Bus stops on or close to the way
55	Dunfermline Ferrytoll Edinburgh	**Edinburgh** *(bus station is 1km from The Way)* **Cramond Brig** **Queensferry** *(south end of the Forth Road Bridge)* **North Queensferry** *(north end of the Forth Road Bridge)* **Inverkeithing** **Rosyth** **Dunfermline**
X59	St Andrews Cupar Glenrothes Edinburgh	**Edinburgh** *(the bus station is 1km from The Way)* **Barnton** *(1km from The Way at Whitehouse Rd)* **Ferrytoll** **St Andrews**
79/79A	Dunfermline Kelty	**Keltybridge** **Kingseat** **Dunfermline**
201/205	Glenrothes Kinross	**Scotlandwell**
66	Glenrothes Auchtermuchty Kinross	**Falkland** **Freuchie**
94/94A	Newburgh Ladybank St Andrews	**Kingskettle** **St Andrews**
64	Glenrothes Ladybank Cupar St Andrews	**Falkland** **Freuchie** **Ceres** **St Andrews**

Transport Websites

Whether you are planning to walk St Andrew's Way in one go or in sections the following websites will be helpful in planning your journey to and from your walk. Bus and train timetables change so make sure you check the up-to-date details before you go.

www.transportdirect.info	An online route/journey planner for public transport and car journeys across Britain
www.travelinescotland.com	Where you can plan any public transport journey within Scotland
www.lothianbuses.com	For bus services in Edinburgh
www.scotrail.co.uk	For train services across Scotland
www.nationalrail.co.uk	National rail enquiries
www.citylink.co.uk	For long distance coach travel across Scotland

Notes